Finance *for* Founders

Finance *for* Founders

The Journey to Unlocking Your Company's Wealth

ROB RIPP

PERFORMANCE
PUBLISHING

**PERFORMANCE
PUBLISHING**

Performance Publishing
McKinney, TX

ISBN:
978-1-961781-85-6 (paperback)
978-1-961781-86-3 (digital cloth hardcover)
978-1-961781-91-7 (case laminate)
978-1-961781-87-0 (ebook)

Library of Congress Control Number: 2025906479

Dedication

To my family, whose unconditional love and support have made so much possible for me.

Table of Contents

Foreword

How I would love to have read this book twenty years ago.

I founded a consulting firm in 2003 and in the early days ran the business, from a financial perspective, by the seat of my pants: client check to client check, paycheck to paycheck. Like many founders, I focused far more on serving clients than the numbers.

Fast forward to 2021. While for many years growth had been slow and lumpy, we had built a fantastic team, a great culture, and a healthy roster of A-list clients. And I was suddenly fielding a steady stream of inquiries from global consultancies, private-equity firms, even individual investors, interested in buying the company.

From those initial conversations it became clear to me that we needed a better, cleaner picture of our finances if we were going to realize the value of what it had taken so long to build. Though our finance capabilities had grown along with the business, our approach to finance was basic, backward-looking, and, frankly, boring. There were certain questions we could not answer with any confidence. Why were our cost of goods sold so low and operating expenses so high? When was the right time to expand our team and what would that cost? What we really needed, and what I knew would be critical to getting us through the next phase of our evolution—and me to the next chapter of my life—was a fractional CFO.

A colleague who had been an audit partner at one of the Big Four recommended that I speak with Rob. And from our first conversation, I knew we were in good hands.

Rob and his team began working with us well before any of my acquisition conversations became serious. They developed a thorough understanding of the business and, in turn, helped us understand how to look at our finances: what was important, where to focus our energy, how to use key metrics to make business decisions. They gave us tools, plans, and metrics along with strategic, actionable advice.

Much of what you'll learn from this book we learned from Rob and the team in real time. Fintelligent was instrumental to our ability to confidently tell the company's story, move with relative ease through due diligence, and successfully close the transaction. And through it all, they were above-and-beyond responsive and brought a positive energy to every interaction. Even during the grind that is due diligence, the team lived their core value to "work joyfully."

As did our work with the Fintelligent team, this book makes clear what I wish I had known from the get-go:

> *Finance is a critical business tool and a lens through which we see how decisions can spur, or hinder, the health and growth of the business.*

In Lindsey's story are the stories of many a founder, myself included. Whether yours is just beginning, or, like Lindsey, you're looking to your next chapter, *Finance for Founders* will empower you to make better decisions for greater growth, profitability, and value.

Kate Rebernak
Founder and CEO, retired
FrameworkESG (acquired by Sodali & Co.)

Acknowledgements

I was inspired to write this book after attending a webinar hosted by Greg Alexander. He's the founder of Collective 54. It's an outstanding mastermind community dedicated to helping founders of boutique professional services firms like me. Being a member has transformed my life. Greg started Collective 54 instead of retiring after selling his company. I'm glad he did. Greg's accomplished great things in his career. His gift is he makes me feel I can accomplish great things, too.

Two people brought this book to life. The first person is my publisher, Michelle Prince of Performance Publishing. Her patience and guidance for this first-time author was invaluable. She motivated me to put in the effort because she was so convincing of the results she's seen with other authors. The next person is Matt Harms, who helped me with the writing. He was instrumental in bringing these characters to life and providing the dialog and flow of the book. I think it makes a dense subject much more readable. This book is not possible without Michelle and Matt.

Finally, I must thank the wonderful founders I have in my life. I work with founders every day and I love it. You are a special group — smart, innovative, a little nutty — that I am proud to serve. There are too many to thank individually on these pages. Suffice it to say that if you knew me when this book was published, you had a hand in its making. Maybe you'll see a little bit of yourself in one of the characters. I hope after reading *Finance for Founders* you'll feel I did right by you.

Introduction

Being a founder is one of the most exhilarating roles on the planet. You're the dreamer, the problem solver, the one who turns a spark of an idea into a thriving business. But if there's one thing I've consistently heard from founders, it's this:

"I didn't start this business to become a better accountant."

This book is for founders like you: brilliant inventors and sharp salespeople whose businesses are scaling, typically bringing in $2 million to $10 million in annual revenue. You're at a pivotal stage where the stakes are higher, decisions carry more weight, and financial missteps can stall your momentum. And yet, like so many founders, you might feel unsure about what's really happening with your numbers.

You may even wonder:

"Are my books a mess? Could I be doing this better?
What am I missing?"

You're not alone. These questions are common and they're not a sign of failure. They're a sign that you're growing.

For many founders, finance feels like a necessary evil—something to tolerate, not leverage. But here's the truth: a well-run financial department isn't just a back-office function. It's a growth engine. It drives profitability, cash flow, and valuation. Finance is the only part of your business that tells you whether your effort is producing real economic returns and can show you how to fix it when it's not.

I know this because I've spent over 25 years exclusively serving owners of growth-stage companies: those looking to break through to the next level. I've seen it all from transformative exits, painful failures, and everything in between. I founded Fintelligent to help founders like you build affordable, high-performing financial functions that support growth and create long-term value. I know what works, what doesn't, and—most importantly—how to help you apply these lessons to your business right now.

If you want proof this approach works, ask an entrepreneur who exited their first company and launched a second. Who did they hire first? More often than not, it was someone to lead finance. They learned the hard way that a great financial team is essential to lasting success.

So why read this book?

It will show you exactly what you need from your financial department to turn your company into a wealth-generating machine.

You'll get free tools from Fintelligent that you can use right away to improve your financial operations. They include templates, key metric calculations and assessments.

And it tells a great story.

You'll follow Lindsey, a founder who built a great business but suffered a financial failure that shook her confidence. Determined not to repeat the mistake, she takes a hard look at her financial operations and transforms not just her business, but her future. Through Lindsey's journey, you'll see how taking control of your financial function isn't about turning you into an accountant (let's be honest, you don't want that and neither do I). It's about gaining clarity, unlocking growth, and achieving both financial and personal freedom.

Why now? Because this is the best moment we've ever had to improve your company's financial capabilities. Cloud-based tools, automation, AI, and a booming outsourcing industry have made world-class financial management accessible, even for small companies. You don't need to wait for a crisis. You can build a better future today.

This book gives you a proven roadmap; one that's been followed by successful entrepreneurs across industries. You'll move from financial uncertainty to confidence, from chaos to clarity. And if you follow through, it might just change your business—and your life—in profound and positive ways.

So, let's get started. Let's take the mystery and frustration out of your financial function and replace it with clarity, confidence, and results. This is your roadmap to unlocking your company's full potential.

Rob Ripp

The Problem

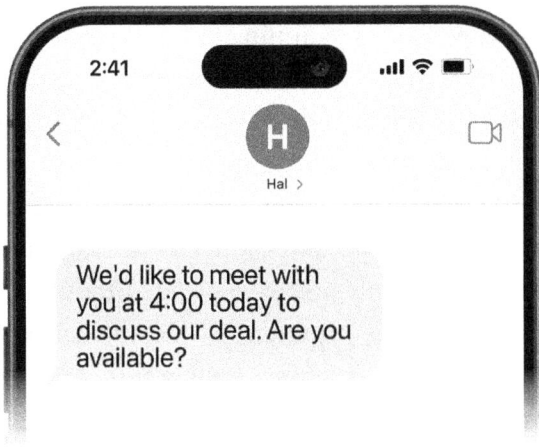

> **2:41** ...ll 🛜 ▮
>
> **H**
> Hal ›
>
> We'd like to meet with you at 4:00 today to discuss our deal. Are you available?

As soon as Lindsey read the text, she knew it was bad news. It wasn't so much the cryptic message, or that Hal wanted to meet in less than two hours.

Hal had never texted her before.

They met over a year ago. Hal was known for buying companies like hers and thought her firm would be a good acquisition. He said all the right things: how they could build a great company together, that she'd be relieved of the daily burdens of business ownership, that she'd have more time to focus on her passion for developing new business and her people. He was known as a hands-off owner and typically maintained his purchases as standalone organizations. The thought of cashing out was intriguing to her and the potential monetary reward would be lucrative.

Lindsey started her business ten years ago after she lost her corporate job. She saw a trend in big companies toward outsourcing certain HR functions, so she started a professional services business offering the very thing that cost her a job. Her old employer was her first customer. Her initial jobs were staffed by her and some independent contractors. Over time, the business grew to about twenty people with almost $5 million in annual revenue. It was profitable and provided a good lifestyle for her, much better than she ever had working for someone else.

She knew she wouldn't be running this business forever, but didn't think about it much because everything was going so well. When Hal came around talking about buying her company, she listened. She spoke with a few friends and colleagues about it, and they were encouraging. She took it upon herself and her staff to negotiate the deal and work through due diligence. Her accounting department was small, consisting of only her ex-coworker Troy, but he had always been the go-to guy in her corporate job, so she felt like she was in good hands with him as her trusted bookkeeper. After Hal sent over a Letter of Intent, Lindsey hired a lawyer to represent her.

When she snapped on her video camera two minutes before the impromptu meeting, Hal and his team were already on the call. She could tell by their faces that they were getting ready to deliver some bad news. Lindsey had Troy with her. Hal started the conversation.

"Lindsey, thanks for taking this call on such short notice. We've been working with you these past few weeks and have come to greatly respect all you've accomplished in building your company. Unfortunately, we can't see how we can go any further with this transaction, so I'm letting you know that we are terminating the LOI we sent to you."

Lindsey was stunned. She knew they'd had some challenges delivering information during due diligence, but they got it done. Hal had said he didn't expect a firm like hers to operate like a larger one and the delays were understandable. She thought he'd be more forgiving when things got difficult. She assumed this call would be a warning, not a termination. After all, she had heard the horror stories of buyers trying to renegotiate terms at the last minute in order to secure a better deal.

"What... what happened?" Lindsey stammered.

"Well, Lindsey, we just don't understand your numbers. We don't think you understand them, either."

Hal wasted no time rattling off a few problems he saw. Bank balances on the balance sheet didn't agree with bank statements. Profit margins were misstated. His biggest issue was the numbers he was told at the start of discussions didn't agree with what his team uncovered during due diligence. In his words, the differences "weren't even close."

They exchanged a few pleasantries, agreed to keep in touch, and concluded the call. Lindsey was embarrassed and humiliated. She was ashamed Hal thought she had such a poor understanding of her finances. She had what she needed to run her business. How else could she have gotten this far?

Hal had mentioned she was running her financials like she was still in her first year of business. He needed to see a robust financial operation he could understand and that would support a rapidly scaling company. "Any buyer would demand that of a standalone acquisition," he said. "We need your financial operation to keep up with where you are going, not where you have been."

The worst part was that, just this week, she had begun to allow herself to think about life after the close. She came from modest means and built a great company. The cash she would have gotten from the exit could have funded her passion for philanthropy. Now it was all gone, and she would have to start over.

About a week after the call, Lindsey came to the realization that at some point she would be exiting her business, with or without Hal. She decided then that it would be on her own terms. Determined to attract the right buyer with the right deal for her, she vowed that the next time she went through an exit process, the outcome would be very different.

Although she couldn't know it at the time, that is exactly what happened. Her next interaction with investors would be very different. And it would change her life.

This is her story of how she got there, with an upgraded financial department leading the way.

* * *

The story of what happened to Lindsey is not at all uncommon in the world of growing businesses. Founders are generally visionaries and passionate about what they do. Almost all founders fall into one of two categories: salespeople and inventors.

The sales-minded founder is focused on reaching the largest market possible and excels at building excitement, forming relationships, and—most importantly—generating sales. The inventor is very much focused on the product or service offered. They are innovators who have a great solution to a problem.

What both types of founders have in common is that they are very good at what they do. If they weren't, chances are they never would have taken the risk to start their own business to begin with. These founders are great at inspiring everyone around them to rally behind the cause and spread the word. The main difference is that sales-minded founders generally spearhead the charge, while innovators surround themselves with great salespeople. These are all great qualities to have, but at some point, they are not going to be enough to grow the business past a certain level of revenue.

Founders often think of themselves as highly versatile. They have to be. In the early days, there is not enough money to support hiring a full team of people needed to cover every possible role. Founders do as much as they can and fill other roles with part-time independent contractors who can perform specific tasks at the lowest possible cost.

This approach works up to a point. The problem is when the company starts to grow beyond the capabilities of the financial team. Many founders admit they know very little about accounting. Since they are uncomfortable with it, they often just get around to it when they can. In the early days they can get away with that attitude. As the company starts to scale, however, the lack of a robust financial operation hinders growth. They need greater financial sophistication to generate ever increasing amounts of cash to fuel growth.

Lots of founders see finances as a necessary evil. Deep down inside they know they should get better at it, but there is nothing sexy about accounting. If there is money in the bank and the taxes are getting paid, the common assumption is that everything is good. Things are even better when the founder can begin to recoup their startup capital. They are at their best when the founder can begin drawing regular distributions that increase substantially each year. And yes, those are all good things. But they are shortsighted as you can see from Lindsey, who was afforded a comfortable lifestyle only to find out everything was not as good as she believed it to be in her business.

The bookkeeper is the person the founder relies on to make sure the basic functions mentioned earlier come to pass. Taxes are paid, bank balances are current, and basic questions about cash flow are answered quickly. A bookkeeper can be the backbone to a new business. Whether they enter on Day 1 or Day 100, they are hired because they have the skills needed to assist the founder with basic accounting functions: classifying transactions, sending reports as needed, and paying bills. Much like Troy, they care and have a vested interest in the success of the company and are happy to continue getting a paycheck. So how did Lindsey wind up where she did with Hal?

Somewhere along the way, the company outgrew Troy. That's not to say Troy just became obsolete overnight. There is still a place for the Troys of the world in a company of any size. Where the problem lies is in the assumption that Troy was able to keep up with the growth of the company. At some point, the finances just became more complex than he was able to handle. He didn't necessarily do anything wrong, he just didn't know what he didn't know. Whatever Lindsey asked for, he provided. Lindsey was so wrapped up in growing her company, she did not notice Troy's role had evolved from that of a bookkeeper, to a controller, and ultimately a CFO. While Troy's role had evolved, his skills had not.

Too often in business the terms for the different roles in a financial department get used interchangeably, which is a problem because they are not all created equal. Look below at the description for each of these roles and then ask yourself if this is how you have your people structured. Chances are you have at least one person in a role they are not qualified for.

Bookkeeper

This is the person who does the day-to-day transaction data entry.

This bookkeeper is trained to follow a process set up by others. They are valued for their attention to detail and for following established procedures. They are not trained to come up with new procedures or to interpret the data they are entering. They can explain why something was booked the way it was, as well as research transactions that need additional clarification.

Accountant

An accountant is responsible for maintaining the integrity of your financial data. They make sure it is accurate and in conformance with Generally Accepted Accounting Principles (GAAP), the set of rules to properly report financials in the US.

Accountant is an enigmatic term people tend to use interchangeably with bookkeeper and controller. Many accountants earned that title because they passed the CPA exam or have many years of experience. A better definition centers on their capabilities. They create processes, interpret accounting rules, assemble financial statements, and ensure an acceptable quality of financial information.

Controller

The controller is the most senior accountant in the organization. They "own" the financial statements, ensuring proper controls and procedures are in place to deliver timely and accurate financials.

A controller generally supervises accountants. They can be an accountant but do not have to be. They develop policies and procedures, holding their staff accountable to them. They can create budgets but are generally not considered "strategic." For example, they may not be able to interpret the financial data to help a founder determine what may—or should—happen next. Controllers are tasked with helping you understand what has happened up until today. They look backward.

Chief Financial Officer

A CFO is a seasoned executive helping the management team allocate resources to maximize return on investment. They are strategic thinkers, tying together disparate information into a cogent set of recommendations that helps a company grow sales, profit, and cash.

This is a broad mandate that requires the CFO to consider quantitative and qualitative data when making recommendations. They have an executive presence needed to handle confidential financial information and hold people accountable for achieving their financial targets. Where a Controller can help a founder understand what happened yesterday and today, the CFO helps you figure out what can happen tomorrow.

> **FINSIGHT**
>
> A Controller helps you understand what happened yesterday and today. A CFO helps you figure out what can happen tomorrow.

2 Key Three Objectives

Lindsey was devastated. The past ten years were spent working long hours to build her business. In the early years she hardly drew a salary and was happy just living off the money from the severance package her company had provided. She thought she was doing a better job of hiding her emotions, but the second Rachel sat down across from her the illusion vanished.

"I guess you weren't kidding when you said you needed a drink!" Lindsey's best friend from college remarked with a degree of concern evident on her own face.

Lindsey took a deep breath while formulating her thoughts, but Rachel did not give her the chance.

"What happened with the sale?"

There it was. Lindsey should have known she could not hide anything from Rachel. Subconsciously, that's probably the reason she invited her out in the first place. "The deal is dead," she said, matter-of-factly. "Can you believe they don't think I know my numbers?"

"Do you?" Rachel asked back in the same straightforward tone Lindsey was using.

Lindsey paused for a moment, surprised by the lack of support in the reply. She sought out Rachel for her business judgment. She ran a division of a much larger company and always spoke of how in her early years she'd get grilled by her managers each month on her numbers. She became so good at managing her business, and her numbers, that she advanced quickly.

Rachel was savvy, however, so she was just going to let Lindsey talk. "I thought I did. But it looks like Hal might have been right. I just learned about an unexpected tax bill. Apparently, I now have to choose between paying the estimated taxes or sending the check for my son's college tuition."

"How can that be?" For the first time Rachel exhibited concern.

"Troy just informed me that the line-of-credit increase we had applied for was declined because the bank felt our overall debt-to-income ratio was too high. That was supposed to help us bridge the gap until the next retainer comes in."

"No. I meant how can you even be in that position? Aren't you doing nearly five million in annual sales?"

Rachel nodded.

"There's been money in the bank the last few months?"

"There was a lot more. Then, we made the decision to get a jump on preparing for that big new client I mentioned to you the last time we spoke. I just heard they pushed back the start date by at least three months, and I am stuck with all the overhead and none of the revenue."

"So, you hired people based on a soft contract start date?" Rachel asked.

"It wasn't supposed to be that way, but yes," Lindsey replied.

Rachel was silent for a moment. She seemed to be searching for the right words in her mind. Instead, she reached into her wallet and placed something on the table covered by her hand. "We go back too far for me to say anything more than this, Lindsey. But I'm willing to bet your financial issues started long before that contract got delayed."

Lindsey's eyes grew wide, unsure if she should defend herself. She chose to stay quiet and listen instead.

"We've had conversations before where you've run into cash problems, but they never had an impact like I'm hearing now. I think that needs to change, quickly, or you may have much bigger problems down the road you can't solve."

"I think you should give this guy Mike a call." Rachel moved her hand off the business card she was covering and pushed it across the table with her fingers. "He runs a company that provides fractional financial departments to entrepreneurs. I know him through a networking group where others have used his firm. They rave about him. Give him a call."

Lindsey took the business card, staring at it like it was from outer space. "What will Troy think if I bring in someone else?"

"You should be more concerned with what Troy, and the other people who work for you, will think when their paychecks stop."

* * *

What Lindsey is learning as she recovers from the initial shock of the events with Hal and Troy is a truth too many founders realize too late. Lindsey had what it took to grow a company from zero to five million dollars. She knows a lot about her business. She also knew she was not qualified to handle the books on her own, which is why she brought on Troy. The executives at her last company went to Troy for everything related to booking transactions and reconciling accounts. He was a logical fit to fill that role in her start up after he also became the same victim of corporate downsizing she had become.

Even with her hands-off approach to accounting, Lindsey thought she was asking the important questions along the way to make sure the finances were healthy. The problem is, she was asking the wrong person. As her accountant, Troy was advising her as he saw things. If she had a CFO, she would have gotten different answers that may have saved her a lot of time, money, and heartache.

Like most founders, Lindsey knew she had three objectives:

1. More cash
2. More sales
3. More profit

More is not an objective. It is far too vague and subjective. What she needed were SMART goals: Specific, Measurable, Achievable, Relevant, and Time-Bound metrics. These become part of a roadmap that eventually results in the Key Three objectives you set. Keeping the Key Three in mind at all times helps founders evaluate tradeoffs as they seek to increase the performance of each objective as part of the overall growth plan.

FINSIGHT

Founders only have three objectives: increasing Cash, Sales, and Profit. Achieve them using SMART goals.

The first category of the Key Three was always the one she stayed most on top of because it was the one that worried her the most: *Cash*. She had no other source of income to fall back on if her company were to run out of money, and she had invested almost everything she had to get it off the ground. As crazy as it sounded for the CEO of a multi-million-dollar company, Lindsey never broke the habit of asking Troy nearly every payroll if there was enough money to cover it. And there always was.

Lindsey did not worry as much about the second objective: *Sales*. This was something that came naturally to her. Many qualified prospects accepted her proposals. Her sales skills were so good that there were points where she had to make the conscious decision to slow down on client acquisition when she didn't have the staff to do the work. That worked for a while when she listened to the experts who advised against staffing ahead for a future demand.

But after a while, she fell into a bad habit of spontaneous hiring because she needed "bodies" to get the work done. She hated losing revenue opportunities and there were bigger costs to cover each month. She loved the continuous sales growth; however, she did not pay attention to the lurking danger of *unprofitable* sales growth. She didn't pay attention because she did not know about it. This would haunt her later.

The third component of the Key Three is where she and many others fail: *Profitability*. The problem is that many founders simply do not know how to properly measure profitability.

An outsourced CFO will often examine the Cost of Goods Sold section of the profit and loss statements (P&L) when taking on a new client. This section is routinely misstated because the founder is not properly capturing labor costs—the cost of people performing work directly for a customer. This is true both for service providers and manufacturers. It's a problem because a founder does not know how much cash is truly left over for overhead and profit once all the customer costs are captured.

An example best illustrates this. Assume the CFO is working with a new client who claims that every dollar of revenue generates ninety cents of gross profit (a 90% gross profit margin), while the CFO knows the industry benchmark is closer to 55%. The client also had a 10% net profit margin, which was below the 20% industry standard.

How can a company with such high gross profit have such low overall profitability?

The answer lies in the gross profit. They were miscalculating it. After doing some work, the CFO determined their gross profit margins were more like 45%. They were getting ten cents less than their peers for every dollar of sales they brought in. They were spending roughly the same 35% on operating expenses like everyone else.

By not knowing their true gross profit, they overestimated their profitability and spent like they were a high-profit-margin business. Their client delivery was inefficient and costing them much more than they realized. This was an issue with the way their business was structured: every single customer they sold to was contributing to this problem. Gross profit needed to increase quickly to prevent further erosion in profits.

Only a CFO would have the experience to recognize this problem and the skill to recommend changes and achievable objectives to fix it. This is where aligning the right people with the right financial problems helps founders better achieve their Key Three objectives.

If you are sensing your business is not as profitable as it should be, you should consult a CFO-level advisor. They should be able to determine quickly if you have a structural issue in your business. They'll also give you ideas you can implement right away to fix it. The good news is the sooner you catch it the easier it is to correct.

This is what Lindsey wanted to explore with Rachel's connection. But she worried: *would she be able to make the right connection that could solve her problems?*

3

The Four Pillars of Every Great Financial Department

"*Knock, knock.*" Lindsey said the words louder than her fingers tapped on the partially ajar door to Troy's office. She knew Troy was as dedicated as they came, but it was still shocking to find him there this late.

Troy, face glued to a spreadsheet on the monitor before him, barely cocked his head to the side to acknowledge her. "Hey, Lindz. How are you holding up?"

"I'll survive." Lindsey stepped into the office to stand over his right shoulder, the perfect angle to shift her focus between the numbers and his facial expression. "But how are you holding up?"

Troy's eyes squinted as his focus on the screen intensified. "Still a little pissed off if I'm being honest." Troy clicked his mouse a few times and the printer beside the monitor hummed to life. "I've been doing this for more than twenty years, almost half of that time with you." Troy took a paper from the printer bed and held it out for Lindsey. "The nerve of this guy to decide in a few weeks that everything is wrong."

"What am I looking at?" Lindsey asked.

"This is our year-to-date profit & loss statement and current balance sheet as of the end of last month. I don't understand why he thinks our numbers are wrong."

Lindsey took a look. Hal had mentioned that bank balances didn't agree with the balance sheet, so she started there. The total cash balance seemed a little high based on what she had in the bank and a couple older, smaller accounts had negative balances. That didn't seem right, and she was surprised she hadn't noticed something so significant before. Why did they have so many bank accounts, anyway? Some of these numbers haven't changed in years.

She flipped through the profit and loss (P&L) statement to find her gross profit. It took her some time but when she found it the amount looked about the same as it always did. She did notice there were an awful lot of accounts on her four-page P&L. The amounts seemed okay to her, even though some were negative amounts. The skepticism on Lindsey's face was unmistakable, but Troy had already shifted his focus back to the monitor. He was now toggling between multiple spreadsheets like a man on a mission.

"Is there a reason you put this together in Excel?" she asked. She'd seen Troy's spreadsheets before. They seemed complex and disjointed to her. She felt like only he really understood them, so she relied on his interpretation rather than studying them herself.

As if struck by sudden paralysis, Troy's fingers stopped moving and his eyes froze in place. "I've been creating reports in Excel for years, why?"

"Didn't we migrate to QuickBooks Online a while back?"

A wave of relief came over Troy. "Yep, and the payroll feature has been a lifesaver. It used to take me a full day to get everyone's check in order but not anymore!" He turned to face her with newfound confidence.

"That's great." Lindsey's voice was barely more than a whisper. "But don't they also have upgraded reporting features to generate these, so you don't have to?" She nodded towards the pages in her hand.

Troy's confidence shifted slightly to one of reproach. "Yeah, but I prefer working in Excel like I always do. It gives me more flexibility. I use QuickBooks to set up all the rules to classify transactions, so we save a lot of time there."

"Got it." Lindsey said, masking her disappointment as best she could. "Why don't you go home and get some rest? It's been a long week." And with that she left the room, hands in her pockets. She touched the card Rachel had given her. She had been carrying it around like it was a pill containing either a cure or poison for her ills.

Lindsey barely slept that night with all the thoughts and questions racing through her mind. Could her business be fundamentally low profit? If so, could that be fixed? She long felt that she'd have to give up some income to finance growth. It had been years of sacrifice, however, and the payoff just wasn't there.

There were a bunch of decisions ahead of her, and she felt a rare sense of anxiety about them. She was never one to shy away from a challenge. Finance was an area she just never felt comfortable with, and that discomfort caused her to dismiss accounting as something to get around to. Those years of delays were now crippling her business. After her experience with Hal, she had resolved that at some point a decision would need to be made to improve her financial function. She thought she'd have more time, but it appeared the time was now. Rachel had never led her astray before. She knew her friend was correct in saying that the future of her employees and company rested in her hands, which made the right choice bigger than any one person.

She was loyal to Troy. He joined her when her business was nothing. To get to the next level she'd have to surround herself with people who were already at the next level. Without thinking, she found her phone was in one hand and Mike's business card was in the other. She was startled when Mike answered.

* * *

"I can't thank you enough for making time to come see me so quickly," Lindsey said with a degree of reverence that caught her by surprise. She had never felt so out of place in the plush leather chair behind the desk in her office. This was her company, and she was used to being in charge, but just the presence of the gentleman now sitting across from her had her feeling unsure of herself.

"Rachel told me it sounded like you have a real problem on your hands. My office is just on the other side of town, so I figured popping in couldn't hurt." Mike was easygoing and pleasant. His casual attire of slacks, an open-collared shirt and a sport coat perfectly complemented his laid-back demeanor. Lindsey was impressed by his approachability. The way Rachel had spoken about him, she was fully expecting the epitome of an accountant to walk through her door: rigid, direct, and a little uptight. This was a pleasant surprise.

"To be honest, I've been torn. But after what you said on the phone about the four pillars, I really felt like you could help us. I've been struggling with how to solve my complete lack of any accounting knowledge whatsoever."

> **FINSIGHT**
>
> **The Four Pillars of every great financial department are Accounting, Reporting, Planning & Analysis, and Advice.**

Mike chuckled. "Don't feel bad. You've just said the first thing 99% of my potential clients say," Mike said with the level of reassurance from someone who had clearly had these types of conversations many times before.

"You've built an incredible company here," Mike motioned to denote the modern office, "and now the goal is to get you a financial operation worthy of your success so you can achieve your highest ambitions for your company."

Something about the words caused a wave of relief to wash over Lindsey. Maybe it was because she didn't have to outright ask for his help, or it could have been his down-to-earth demeanor. It was most likely that she didn't feel judged. He spoke like he dealt with problems like hers all the time. She was still hesitant—this was a big deal for her. There was no turning back now. "Tell me how this works."

Mike pulled out a small tablet and flipped open the cover. He took a second to review his notes before returning his attention to

Lindsey. "From what you told me on the phone, this potential buyer found almost a million-dollar discrepancy in your gross profit?" he asked without expression while still scanning the notebook.

"That's what they said…" Lindsey felt foolish. *How could she not know this?*

"Okay. I reviewed the profit and loss statement you sent to them. I think I know what their problem is."

He went on: "There are no labor costs in your Cost of Goods Sold. Professional service providers like your company have staff who perform work directly for clients. You can't collect revenue without that work. In that case, we recognize those labor costs so we can see how much profit remains to cover overhead and owner income. There are likely other costs missing as well."

He told her this was important to investors like Hal. They see a lot of deals. She's competing with those other deals for Hal's investment. Hal evaluates deals by analyzing the company's financial statements. It's why financial statements were invented: to give investors and lenders a consistent way to evaluate different companies.

She had two problems. First, she told Hal her gross profit was higher than it was, which damaged her credibility. The next problem was that when he compared Lindsey's books to others, it was clear her books were not properly prepared. That was too much risk for Hal, so he decided to move forward with his other opportunities.

This made sense to Lindsey. Mike was direct, but easy in his delivery. He reminded her of her beloved high school track coach.

"Now, this is just one observation. We'd need to do an assessment to see what else needs to get cleaned up and what happens next."

"That sounds reasonable," Lindsey said. "What does that look like?"

"Let me start by saying that my company provides an outsourced solution. It's different from consulting. Are you aware of the difference?"

"Not really."

"It's simple. As outsourcers, we recommend improvements, then implement and maintain them. We become part of your team. Consultants will recommend improvements but leave it up to you and your team to implement."

Lindsey thought this through. She was warming to Mike and could see how the regular presence of competent financial professionals could really elevate her company. It didn't sound cheap, and she wasn't sure she was ready to take on more cost. There also was Troy to consider. She'd have to get much more comfortable with the benefits Mike and his team would bring to her company before signing on.

The Four Pillars

Mike started by saying that his firm works exclusively with firms in her growth stage. He then explained that every great financial department does four things very well. He called them the four pillars:

- **Accounting:** Getting your foundational financial data right.
- **Reporting:** Gaining insights from your data and communicating performance to others.
- **Planning & Analysis:** A roadmap and analytics to drive continuous financial improvement.
- **Advice:** An expert providing their knowledge and strategic guidance to scale your business.

Mike explained the sequence of implementation, with accounting being where it all begins. If the data isn't correct, everything else is useless. They then implement the other pillars based upon the client's needs and budget. He recommended starting here, then expanding into the other pillars.

Lindsey liked the approach. It seemed to offer a lot of flexibility and would certainly solve some of her immediate problems while providing a roadmap to tackling her longer-term issues. She had one concern.

"I have an accountant on my staff. His name is Troy. He's been with me since the start. How would you work with him?"

"That's great to hear," said Mike. "We like to have a point of contact who is not the founder to help us with the day-to-day activities. I think he'll like working with us. We'll introduce new processes and systems to automate his work and make his life easier. If he's open to some coaching, maybe we can help him build some new skills and he can help you in even better ways."

"Troy takes a while to warm up to new ideas, but once he buys in, he's all in," said Lindsey. She was glad Troy would have a role going forward and intrigued that he could continue to develop his career with her company.

"How do we get started?" Lindsey asked.

"We're going to connect to your accounting system to perform an assessment of your current situation. We'll give you a report of what we observed and some recommendations for improvement. This will aid your research as you figure out how you want to solve your problem."

We have two next steps. First is you enable us access to your accounting systems. Next is to set a date for the assessment. Think we can take care of this now?"

"On it!" said Lindsey.

ASSESSMENT: THE FOUR PILLARS

Rate yourself on the following questions according to how satisfied you are with each. Insert a number between one and ten in each box and add them up. One means you are very dissatisfied; ten means you are very satisfied.

1. How satisfied are you with the accuracy of your financial data? _____

2. How satisfied are you with the delivery speed of your financial data? _____

3. How satisfied are you with the way your financial data is being reported and communicated? _____

4. How effectively does your financial reporting help you understand the performance of your business? _____

5. How well does your financial department use data to identify and address areas for improvement? _____

6. How well do your financial reports inform decision-making within the company? _____

7. How effective is your company's financial planning and analysis in providing a roadmap for continuous performance improvement? _____

8. How satisfied are you with the level of strategic guidance you receive from your financial department? _____

9. How confident are you in the financial department's ability to scale the business and deliver increased sales, profits, and cash flow?

10. How satisfied are you with the overall effectiveness of your financial department in achieving business goals? _____

Add up your score and write it here: _____

INTERPRETATION

Score Range: 10 to 60

Needs Improvement

You may need to invest more time and resources in building up your financial department.

Score Range: 61 to 80

Neutral

You have a functioning financial department but may benefit from refining processes or improving certain areas.

Score Range: 81 to 100

Strong Financial Department

You have a strong financial department in place, with good control over accounting, reporting, planning, and advice.

Scan code to take the Four Pillars assessment online
https://finforfounders.com/four-pillars

4

Pillar 1: Accounting

Lindsey sat in front of the video conference waiting room screen within the confines of her own office, a mix of anxiety and anticipation beginning to take root as she waited. She knew she needed to do better and wanted to be better at financial matters. Like waiting for a high school exam result, she was anxious about what the assessment would say about her business. And by extension, her management of it.

The thought of jointly taking the call from the same room with Troy had crossed her mind, but with all the other unknowns surrounding what was about to take place she had decided that a comfortable distance between them would be for the best.

"Nice to see everyone this morning," Mike said confidently. After exchanging some pleasantries, he launched the agenda and shared his desktop. "Troy, it's a pleasure to meet you. I understand Lindsey explained to you why we are here and what we hope to accomplish. My role is to oversee this entire process. I've brought into this meeting my colleague, Julien. She is one of our excellent Virtual Accountants. Should we work together, she will be your point of contact. Her role is to make sure your company's foundational financial data is accurate, timely and easy to get."

"Thanks, Mike," Julien chimed right in with the precision of someone who had clearly done this more than a few times. "Lindsey, it's great to finally meet you. And Troy, thank you for being a part of this process. You and I are going to be working together closely should Lindsey choose to move forward with us after our assessment."

Lindsey couldn't see Troy below the neck, but based on his facial expression she could tell he was uncomfortable. "Thank you both for making the time to get this started so quickly for us," Lindsey embraced her CEO role and pushed Troy's feelings to the back burner for the time being. "Let us know what you need to get started and Troy will get it right to you."

"You already enabled our access to QuickBooks Online, so that's great." Mike took control of the call once more. "What I'd like to do first is show you a report of our findings, as well as a sample of what your new financial reporting could look like."

As Mike continued his review, Lindsey could feel Troy getting more defensive. Too many times, he chimed in explaining why things appeared a certain way. He didn't seem to be on board with the way things would change if Lindsey adopted this new approach. Julien handled Troy's concerns professionally. She explained that what they evaluated was very common for businesses like Lindsey's. They had great success boosting the financial performance of clients using the approach they were discussing now. The increased clarity into their firm's financial performance helped founders make crisper, more informed decisions.

It was clear to Lindsey that working with Mike would be the way to go. The way they quickly uncovered the problems she was having combined with their practical solutions just made sense to her. She could see the value in it immediately. But she had two big concerns:

1. Would Troy buy into this new approach? He was key to successfully implementing it.

2. Was she ready to make the investment in money and time? She would have to confront her fears around financial matters—there would be no more hiding from it.

* * *

For all the things Lindsey had accomplished in business, she was slightly embarrassed at how nervous she was feeling when the end of the day rolled around. After the earlier call with Mike and Julien ended, she left Troy alone to give him time to process everything. Usually after meetings like this Troy would reach out. A phone call or text. A question or protest about the process. But there had been nothing but silence.

Lindsey checked her email and saw the follow-up notes from the meeting. Mike had provided a recording of the meeting, an AI transcription, and the report they just presented. She flipped through the report and soon found herself engrossed in its presentation. Scorecards, charts, and tables neatly presented as key data. A sleek, streamlined profit and loss statement popped up on her screen. If not for the title at the top of the page she might not have even known what she was looking at in comparison to the reports she was accustomed to getting from Troy.

She emailed Mike back, asking for a time to meet. He responded with some times and dates. They settled on one in a couple days. When the time came, Lindsey hopped on the call to see Mike and Julien waiting.

"Good to see you, Lindsey," Mike said. "I'd like to get your feedback on what we've discussed so far."

"Thanks, Mike. I reviewed the report, and I have a question. What happened to all the other line items on the P&L? These reports used to be four or five pages long." Lindsey became concerned for a moment that important information had been overlooked.

"We consolidated your chart of accounts in a more efficient way," Mike said. "We can get into more detail another time, but as an example, take a look at the grouping for employee compensation and benefits." He paused until it looked like Lindsey had located the correct spot. "In your old P&L reports, this was split into more than a dozen smaller categories like: payroll, medical insurance, and a whole bunch of state payroll tax accounts. We consolidated accounts to make it easier to read. Now you can quickly see the entire investment in your people. We'll create supplemental reports with more detailed information should you want to see that."

"And where did all my bank account information go?" Lindsey asked while staring at a single line item under assets where the word "Cash" was listed. "We had diversified to several different institutions after the financial crisis."

"Same premise as the expenses, Lindsey." Mike was obviously happy with her questions and interest in understanding more of what they were doing. "We totaled everything up for this report to make it easier to read. Those supplemental reports I just mentioned will provide you with more detail. We also have some ideas on consolidating your accounts to make things easier for you, as well as upgrading your banking relationship to earn interest on those balances."

"Wow," said Lindsey, impressed with how quickly Mike and Julien were able to reimagine her P&L. "It's like you waved a magic wand and gave me the report I needed to see. I feel like this would have taken us forever to generate, if at all."

Mike explained, "Over the coming weeks we are going to reimagine your entire reporting system to provide you insights that are more organized and easier to read. But first, we do have a couple more items we would like to go over with you."

"I'm all ears," Lindsey said while taking out a notepad to make sure she didn't miss anything.

"Have you noticed that there are some months where you are wildly profitable and others where you are losing money?" From the countless times he had had this exact same conversation with a business owner, Mike could predict what she was about to say and continued. "Yes, business has its ups and downs. But we are talking about big month-to-month swings."

"A lot of those swings are because of payment delays," Lindsey explained. "We have been making electronic payments a requirement for new clients and doing our best to migrate existing customers away from paying by check, but we don't want to rock the boat too much since they do always pay." Lindsey was confident in her logic.

"I can see how that could have an impact…" Mike was quiet for a second while choosing his next words carefully. Despite having had this conversation countless times he was very conscious of throwing too much information at her too quickly. "But the lag time in receiving payments from your good customers should never be a reason for your P&L to vary so much. It has more to do with the accounting basis Troy is using: cash versus accrual. We are going to review that as well and can take a deeper look on our next call."

"That sounds wonderful." Lindsey was obviously relieved to know there was a simple fix, especially one she was not going to have to deal with right now. She had heard of cash and accrual accounting but didn't really know what it meant.

"The last thing I wanted to speak to you about today is the process you currently have for your monthly close."

"Monthly close?" Lindsey thought she had heard incorrectly for a second. "Do you mean our quarterly reports?"

Mike and Julien paused for a moment. "Quarterly reports are great," Mike began, "but you need better visibility. If there is something amiss, we want to catch it sooner. You should be closing your books and issuing reports each month."

"We think improving this process will validate your data and streamline your financial system," Julien jumped in to finish Mike's thought as they so often did with each other. "This is something we really want to address as soon as possible to ensure your financial statements are being prepared correctly and that you are getting the most accurate, timely data."

"Okay, how do we do that?" Lindsey had been very impressed with everything Mike's company had done for her thus far and was not about to start pushing back now.

"First, we create a process and checklist to properly close the books and document it. We'll train Troy on what he does and what we do. Next, we create a review process so that a second set of eyes can review the close and question anything that does not seem proper. This is done by a member of our team. This secondary level of review is critical to ensure we have good data."

Lindsey was apprehensive. She said "Troy usually handled all this himself. I'm not sure how he will handle this new bureaucracy. It seems like this will be a lot of extra work."

Julien said "Documentation gives us something to measure against our close process. We want to do things efficiently and accurately." My team is measured by how well they close the books, so we use these metrics to ensure we deliver quality service to you. I think once you and Troy get into the flow of things, you'll see how well this new process will work for you."

A wave of relief washed over Lindsey. In a way, she was excited to take a step back in anticipation of what new view of her company she would get to see this time. "Just tell me what time works best for you both and I will make sure Troy is there!"

Cash Versus Accrual

Many founders have heard of cash basis versus accrual basis accounting and aren't sure what it means. The simplest explanation is that accrual basis accounting matches the timing of revenue and expenses, whereas cash basis accounting does not. Companies should use accrual basis accounting to manage their books. Matching revenue with expense in the period when it occurs helps you evaluate your profitability, return on investment, and so much more. Those same companies may use cash basis accounting to prepare their tax returns. This ensures there is enough cash to pay any tax liabilities.

> **FINSIGHT**
>
> **Accrual basis accounting matches the timing of revenue and expenses; cash basis does not.**

Cash basis accounting involves accounting for transactions at the time cash changes hands without regard for the timing of when. Many companies bill their revenue and collect the cash later, sometimes as long as ninety days later. During that time, expenses are being paid. This mismatch can really distort a company's profitability.

This is best illustrated by example. Assume a company incurs $75,000 of costs, paid out at $25,000 per month for a specific customer. They bill the customer $100,000 which is paid in ninety days. The cash basis P&L would look like this:

	Month 1	Month 2	Month 3	Total
Revenue			$100,000	$100,000
Expenses	25,000	25,000	25,000	75,000
Profit	(25,000)	(25,000)	75,000	25,000

Each month when you got your cash-basis P&L, you'd see a $25,000 loss for a couple months, then a $75,000 profit. You know this is not correct—when you bid on the job you knew you would earn $25,000. The problem is that you had to wait three months and view a quarterly P&L to know this. That's too long. Your profitability is distorted because the timing is off. Multiply this scenario by the number of transactions in your company and you can quickly see how cash basis accounting distorts your financials.

Here's the same example using accrual accounting:

	Month 1	Month 2	Month 3	Total
Revenue	$100,000			$100,000
Expenses	75,000			75,000
Profit	25,000	0	0	25,000

Now your revenue and expenses are recorded in the same period in which they occur. You can measure how profitable the business is and not have to wait until the end of the quarter to do so.

Businesses use cash basis accounting for many reasons, but there are generally two that account for most situations. The first is that business owners who serve as their own bookkeepers like to track their cash. It makes logical sense to record an expense when the money leaves the account and record income when the money arrives.

The second reason is due to the tax preparer who usually sets up the books for a new company. Virtually all new companies pay taxes on a cash basis. They want to earn the cash they use to pay their taxes. It also makes it easier for the accountant to prepare tax returns.

The objective should not be about easier tax return preparation. It should be about accuracy and transparency.

For an owner to properly manage their business, the books must be kept on an accrual basis. It is the only way to properly measure financial performance because you are matching the timing of income and expense. When you organize your books in such a way it provides a much clearer insight as to what it truly costs to run the business. With a firm grasp on your actual profitability, you are then making proper decisions about allocating resources to generate the best returns.

Another reason why you need to use accrual accounting is for tracking key performance indicators. Doing it on a cash basis will give you bad data, leading to bad outcomes from your decisions.

Converting from cash to accrual accounting involves several steps. This is something many accountants perform for companies in their earlier stages of growth when it can be accomplished in a reasonable amount of time and cost. Don't be intimidated by a service provider who quotes you a high cost to convert your basis—you may be paying for much more than you need.

Keep in mind that you are not keeping two sets of books or doing anything that might seem unethical. You are tracking your *basis*. Your day-to-day bookkeeping will move on to an accrual basis, but your tax returns can still be submitted on a cash basis to ensure you only pay taxes on your cash transactions. Your tax preparer will complete a schedule on your corporate tax return called *Schedule M-1 — Reconciliation of Income (Loss) per Books with Income (Loss) per Return.* This reconciles your books to your tax return. If you are ever audited, the auditor will use this schedule to vouch your books. Just make sure nothing has changed in your books since you prepared your tax return.

While the complexity will vary, here's generally what's involved in converting from cash to accrual basis:

1. **Establish accounts receivable.**
   Create invoices for all unpaid customer revenue earned but not yet paid. Put them on the balance sheet.

2. **Set up prepaid expenses.**
   Record expenses that were paid in advance but not yet used. For example, if you paid for a twelve-month insurance policy, only include the portion used up during the period.

3. **Create accounts payable.**
   Prepare bills for all vendors who have provided a product or service that you have not yet paid.

4. **Accrue expenses.**
   Record items where you have incurred the expense but have not yet incurred it or been billed for it. This could be things like interest payable, deferred revenue, or client costs incurred but not yet billed.

The Chart of Accounts

The Chart of Accounts (COA) is a structured list of an organization's financial accounts, essential for organizing transactions within a company's general ledger (the main accounting record of a company). This system categorizes transactions into accounts such as assets, liabilities, equity, revenues, and expenses, which help in creating and interpreting financial statements. A well-designed Chart of Accounts provides a clear, customizable framework for recording and reporting financial data, ensuring accuracy and compliance with financial regulations. For growth-stage companies, an effective COA is vital as it allows for streamlined financial tracking, better financial management, and informed decision-making, which are crucial for scaling operations and enhancing profitability.

As we can see from Lindsey's interaction with Mike and Julien, she knew what the chart of accounts was, but did not know how it could be used to best work for her. This is not uncommon for founders, and quite common in organizations where financial complexity has surpassed the ability of their original bookkeeper. In the early days of the company, there was no harm in creating a new account when something new had to be recorded and the user was not sure how to do it. Over time "when in doubt, create an account" no longer works because account proliferation has made the Chart of Accounts a mess.

The Chart of Accounts is organized based on the sections of financial statements. At the top are asset accounts on the balance sheet. After balance sheet accounts come profit and loss statement accounts. This section can get large quickly.

Lindsey noted that her P&L was very long. Troy was creating an account for everything. There were over eight accounts listing out various jurisdictions to remit employer payroll taxes. Besides taking up too much space, listing these payroll expense accounts do not help Lindsey better manage her business. These are not *controllable* costs for her. They are costs associated with gross wages, which are controllable. A better approach would be to consolidate employer payroll taxes into a single line item, then group accounts into meaningful sections that are controllable so Lindsey can decide how she wants to invest in her business—and more easily calculate the returns on that investment.

FINSIGHT

Group subaccounts into meaningful categories. This better tracks and measures investments in your company and their return.

Updating the chart of accounts is a straightforward process, but also one that can cause a lot of headaches if not done properly. Here are some things to keep in mind if you want to try it yourself:

1. **Create an account map first in a spreadsheet.**
   This simply maps your old accounts to the new ones. It will help you stay organized.

2. **Use account numbers.**
   This gives each account a unique code, making transaction classification easier and more accurate. Next time someone says, "book it to travel," you can say, "you mean account 53000 Meals & Entertainment?" Travel could mean different things to different people and using numbers ensures you have a common language.

3. **Create relevant account groupings on your profit and loss statement.**
   Want to know the cost of your workforce? Create an account called "Compensation and Benefits" and create separate subaccounts for Gross Wages, Employer Payroll Taxes, Employee Benefits, etc. Those accounts will sum to a total Compensation and Benefits grouping. You now have the amount you spend on your workforce.

You can modify your P&L report to show what percentage of revenue you spend on Comp & Benefits and then compare it to other companies in your industry. You can also collapse subaccounts into a parent account to provide a clean summary P&L which is great for sharing with others.

Here is an example of accounts that have been realigned:

PRIOR CHART OF ACCOUNTS	REALIGNED CHART OF ACCOUNTS
Advertising/Promotional	50000 Compensation & Benefits
Payroll expense	51000 Gross Wages
Payroll Taxes	52000 Incentive Compensation
Payroll Expenses NJ SUI	53000 Employer Paid Payroll Taxes
Payroll Expenses State of NJ	54000 Employee Benefits
FUTA Tax	**Total 50000 Compensation & Benefits**
Health Insurance	60000 Sales & Marketing Expenses
Total Payroll Expenses	60100 Content Creation
Networking Events	60200 Digital Advertising
Automobile Expenses	60300 Marketing Events
Meals and Entertainment	**Total 60000 Sales & Marketing Expenses**
Travel	70000 Travel & Entertainment
Lodging	71000 Travel & Lodging
Airfare	72000 Meals & Entertainment
Total Travel	**Total 70000 Travel & Entertainment**

Scan code to download a sample chart of accounts
https://finforfounders.com/chart-of-accounts

Monthly Close

The monthly close process is a critical accounting procedure for any company, particularly for those in the growth stage, as it ensures that financial records are accurate and up-to-date. This process involves reconciling all accounts, verifying transaction details, and ensuring all financial entries for the month have been properly recorded. The goal is to have accurate, verifiable financial data available to produce reliable financial statements. A disciplined monthly close process helps identify discrepancies, manage cash flow effectively, and prepare for audits. This fosters a robust financial structure that supports sustainable growth.

The term "monthly close" comes from the early days of accounting. Transactions were kept in handwritten books. Each book contained transactions for a single account. These transactions were summed at the end of a month. Each book's sum was transferred to another handwritten book called the "general ledger." After those entries were completed the general ledger was "closed" and the data transferred to financial statements.

Modern technology now automates this process, yet many founders don't know how monthly close happens. Following these practices will introduce enough discipline and oversight to ensure accurate preparation of financial statements.

There are generally seven steps to the process.

1. **Set a closing schedule.**
   Establish a clear timeline for when financial statements should be issued each month. Work backward to determine the schedule of activities needed to achieve the deadline. Communicate dates and tasks to all relevant team members to ensure everyone understands their responsibilities and the timing.

2. **Document the process.**
   Maintain detailed documentation of the close process, including who performed each task and when. Keep a

checklist of tasks. This documentation is crucial for audits and for refining the closing process over time.

3. **Collect and review financial data.**
   Maintain an electronic set of workpapers. These workpapers include various types of information: documents, spreadsheets, correspondence, receipts, and statements—anything that provides a detailed audit trail that justifies everything found in a financial statement. Keep it well-organized in an online document management system.

4. **Reconcile accounts.**
   Perform reconciliations of all major accounts, especially bank, credit card, and merchant accounts. This involves matching the balances in the accounting records against external sources like bank statements to confirm accuracy.

5. **Prepare adjusting entries.**
   Make any necessary adjusting entries to account for accruals, depreciation, amortization, and other accounting adjustments that reflect the true financial position of the business for the month.

6. **Review the work.**
   After the team has completed their work, a supervisor (usually an accounting manager or the Controller) will review everything. They may perform an "analytical review," which is simply comparing balances from one month to the next. They will question anything that is out of order.

7. **Close the books.**
   After all questioned items are settled, the supervisor will sign off and finalize all entries for the month. The entries are entered into your accounting software. After the books are closed, lock the period in your accounting software to prevent further changes to the records. This maintains data

integrity by preventing history from changing. Nothing is more frustrating than sharing a financial report with someone only to find it no longer matches what is in your accounting software!

FINSIGHT

Here's a tip to make sure your accountants are on top of things.

At the end of a month, fetch the bank reconciliation reports for all your bank and credit card accounts. Review the "uncleared" section.

If you see any deposits more than five days old or withdrawals more than thirty days old, ask your accountant why. Those items may be misstating your cash.

You may hear the terms "soft close" and "hard close." A soft close is a more cursory review where the accountant just posts transactions and prepares bank reconciliations. A hard close is a more detailed review where the accountant reviews all accounts and makes adjusting entries to ensure financials are properly stated. Some companies do hard closes each quarter. We recommend hard monthly closes.

We believe accountants should always maintain "audit-ready" books. These are financial records that would pass an audit from an independent accounting firm. In other words, your financials are free from any material misstatements.

A proper monthly closing might be one of the most elusive parts of the accounting process we see with growing businesses. Very rarely do banks or investors ask to see any documentation of how the close works, since the standard request is for financial statements. They assume the close is acceptable until proven otherwise. If they are proven otherwise, they can quickly lose confidence in your numbers and terminate a deal you wanted for your business.

Without having a regular cadence around the monthly close the risk of making errors increases. Accounting is unceasing. Good systems require regular care and maintenance to keep the flow of data updated and accurate. Having a proper monthly close process in place might not have been enough on its own to prevent Lindsey from losing her deal with Hal. It is likely that a better process would have identified problems earlier and made her financials more accurate before presenting them to a prospective investor.

Scan code to download a monthly close checklist
https://finforfounders.com/close-checklist

ASSESSMENT: ACCOUNTING

Rate yourself on the following questions according to how satisfied you are with each. Insert a number between one and ten in each box and add them up. One means you are very dissatisfied; ten means you are very satisfied.

1. How satisfied are you with the accuracy and organization of your Chart of Accounts? _____

2. How confident are you that your accounting system properly categorizes transactions into relevant accounts? _____

3. How satisfied are you with the clarity and relevance of your financial statements (e.g., balance sheet, income statement)? _____

4. How confident are you in your understanding of the differences between cash basis and accrual basis accounting? _____

5. How satisfied are you with your current accounting method (cash versus accrual) and its ability to provide accurate financial insights? _____

6. How effective is your monthly close process in ensuring accurate and timely financial data? _____

7. How confident are you that your reconciliations for bank, credit card, and merchant accounts are accurate and up-to-date? _____

8. How satisfied are you with your process for identifying and correcting accounting discrepancies? _____

9. How satisfied are you with your team's ability to catch mistakes before they get to you? _____

10. How confident are you that your accounting function is "audit-ready" and free from material misstatements? _____

Add up your score and write it here: _____

INTERPRETATION

Score Range: 10 to 60
Accounting Rebuilders

Your accounting function may require significant improvement.
It's essential to invest time and resources to establish a reliable
accounting foundation.

Score Range: 61 to 80
Accounting Builders

Your accounting function has a good foundation
but needs some refinement. Consider targeted investments
to address key weaknesses.

Score Range: 81 to 100
Accounting Champions

Your accounting function is strong, and you likely do not need
significant investments. Focus on continuous improvement
and maintaining standards.

Scan code to take the Accounting assessment online
https://finforfounders.com/accounting

5

Pillar 2: Reporting

Lindsey strolled through the office with coffee in one hand and her laptop in the other. With every office and cubicle she passed, her employees poked their heads up to take notice. Some offered a nod, others a smile, and there were even a few full "good mornings." They sensed her tension over the past month. It seemed to be easing. The extra greetings were a test of her mood.

Her mood was much better, and for good reason. The atmosphere in the entire office had been noticeably different over the course of the last thirty days. No one knew much about the work she had been doing with Mike and his team, but it was clear she seemed much less burdened than she was a month ago.

"How's it going, Troy?" Lindsey poked her head into his office and asked with such an upbeat tone that caught Troy by surprise. For once he was not buried at a desk full of paperwork but was instead engrossed in something on his computer screen.

But she was not the only one. "Hey, Lindz." He smiled at her with more confidence and joy she had seen in a very long time. "Everything is great."

"Really?" Lindsey couldn't hide a hint of surprise.

"Yeah, really." Troy motioned for Lindsey to come join him. "Do you know that we have had increasing revenue every month for the past six months? Last month was our biggest in the last twelve."

It took a second for Lindsey to process what Troy was saying as she stared at a neatly organized grouping of charts on his screen. "How'd you figure all this out?"

"I didn't," Troy said proudly. "This is all on the dashboard Mike and Julien created. But as I spend less time on some of the tasks they automated I've been watching some great videos they gave me on processes and how to use the reports they create."

Lindsey leaned over his shoulder to confirm for herself what he was saying was correct. She felt relieved that Troy accepted the changes the company was making. She was also impressed by his newfound desire to learn more in areas he had never focused on before. "I love it, Troy. Please let me know if there is anything else I can do to help you." She patted him on the back and spun on her heels with a spring in her step.

After the pit stop at Troy's office, Lindsey continued toward her own. She still had a few minutes before her scheduled meeting with Mike and Julien, but she wanted to be fully situated and ready to absorb what was about to happen.

Mike had done a great job of preparing for what was to come next. Lindsey was impressed with what she had seen so far and was eager to hear the latest developments. It was still a little unsettling to realize how little she knew about her finances. She got past that as she realized how powerful this new wealth of knowledge would be in scaling her business.

"Lindsey!" Mike said with a smile after she clicked the "join" button on her video conference. They were both two minutes early.

Lindsey took a second to look from Mike to Julien, then recentered on both. "Do you guys do everything with this much precision?" she asked, thinking back to too many meetings with countless wasted hours spent waiting for a host to start a meeting.

"Ha!" Mike chortled. "We do. We know how important finances are to our clients and want to make sure they know that by running great meetings. We like to keep it tight."

"Do you have the link I emailed earlier?" Julien asked.

"Sure do," Lindsey said, while clicking her mouse a few times. "Okay, I'm in." Lindsey paused as information populated on the screen until she found herself looking at a quadrant with four data sets: YTD

Revenue, Direct Labor Hours, Monthly Burn Rate, and Gross Profit Margins. Each indicator was on a scorecard comparing the current amount to the prior period, along with a monthly trendline. Lindsey was impressed at how this new way of looking at her data communicated so much so quickly.

"What do you think?" Mike asked.

"All the numbers seem to be positive, so that's good, right?" Lindsey was a little overwhelmed by seeing the overview of her entire business laid out in front of her so concisely.

"It's a good start for sure," Julien took control of the call again. "But there are definitely areas we can improve based on what we tend to see in other professional service firms."

"Where would you start?"

"Take a look at your gross profit margins. Remember earlier we said that your margins were too high? We had to allocate to your cost of revenue the labor costs when your staff worked on your clients' projects. After we did that, your gross profit margins are only 45%, which is far below the industry average of 60%. This means the projects you do for your customers are not as profitable as you thought they were. We looked into it, and it seems too much work is being done by your senior people, who are the most expensive."

"Really? It seems like everyone is always so busy and there is still work left to be done. That's why we went through the last round of hiring." Lindsey was struggling to comprehend how she could do more with less.

"If your direct labor costs were more in line with what they should be," Julien continued without addressing Lindsey's concern, "then your gross profit margin would look more like this."

Lindsey inhaled deeply as Julien shared an image of her screen. It showed her gross profit margin at the target of 60%. Adding 15% more profit margin to her $5 million business added $750,000 to her gross profit! That was just for this year. With a few taps, Julien updated her forecast for next year. The increase was over $1 million.

"How did you do this so quickly?" Lindsey asked.

"Click refresh on your browser," Julien responded. She waited until Lindsey did as instructed. When she could tell that they were both looking at the same numbers she said, "These reports are updated in real time. All we need to do is change one of the inputs, and the program will recalculate everything that is impacted by the change. It is a great tool for helping forecast and decide where the best return is on your investment."

"I used to have to wait a long time to get updates like this, and wade through a giant Excel spreadsheet. By the time I got it the data was out of date. We have never been able to forecast like this before," Lindsey replied.

"Lots of things are going to be different, Lindsey," Mike said as Julien stopped screen sharing so his face could take center stage. "All this is going to help us reshape your annual financial plan based on what your P&L will look like a year from now."

"Mike, this is great. I love it. Can you walk me through what that's going to look like?" This was the first time she could ever remember looking forward to financial reports.

"It's going to look very much like these scorecards and dashboards you see here, which is very different from what Troy was doing with spreadsheets," Mike replied. "We filter out the numbers that don't matter, although we can make them available to you with other reports. You won't have to wade through dense spreadsheets that take too long to create and break too easily."

Julien was typing away on her computer with a grin while addressing Lindsey. "If we run some projections for your operating income at the end of the year based on all the changes we have made so far, and ones that we will continue making over the next few months, I think you will be pleasantly surprised."

Suddenly, a screenshare appeared in the meeting. Lindsey found herself looking at a close-up view of a line titled EBITDA. The dollar amount was higher than what she was used to seeing. "You really think this is doable?"

"I do. We've implemented the same recommendations at other clients and the results have been dramatic," Mike asserted. "The important thing is to stick to the plan and, if things are not working as planned, identify them and pivot quickly to something that works better."

"I think I'd be crazy not to!" Lindsey laughed.

"That's good." Mike took the opportunity to seize Lindsey's excitement, knowing he would need the momentum on his side for the more difficult conversations they needed to have. "But before we can get there we need to address some of the bigger issues we found. The good news is that these are solvable problems and should clear up a lot of the confusion you had with your line of credit extension."

"Okayyyy," Lindsey sighed as she sat back in her chair and waited for Mike to continue.

"What do you notice about this balance sheet?" Mike asked.

Lindsey placed her elbows on the desk and leaned in close. "I see some negative numbers in the cash category. That doesn't seem right. Wouldn't that mean my bank accounts are overdrawn?"

Julien appeared to do a double take as if surprised by Lindsey's answer. "You're correct! Are they overdrawn?"

"No," Lindsey said.

"Also correct," explained Julien. "But these are the financial statements you gave the bank. When they saw these negative balances they assumed that your banking was not up to date. They concluded that your financials were inaccurate, so they could not determine your liquidity or ability to take on more debt."

"That explains why that last loan was declined." Lindsey muttered the words under her breath, but still loud enough for Mike to hear.

"Definitely a big contributor." Julien also noticed the time ticking by and moved to wrap up the call. "There are other things we found. If it's okay with you, we are just going to rework everything for you to review on our next call."

The relief on Lindsey's face was evident. She nodded her agreement and eagerly got back to focusing on the parts of her business she enjoyed.

Financial Statements

Having information without context is not enough. You need to have the right information at the right time and to be able to understand what it is really telling you. This was true in Lindsey's case. Troy provided her with information. As the business grew, Troy struggled to keep up by doing more of what he was doing before. It was too manual and proved to not be enough; the complexities of the business demanded an upgrade to the finance function's capabilities. He struggled to present the information in a clear and concise manner for Lindsey to easily digest.

Like most founders, Lindsey was busy and had to prioritize where she spent her time. When dissecting a report took too long she took quick glances at what she thought was important and assumed everything was in good order. As she was not confident in her financial acumen, she pushed it off and focused on other things. She delegated financial matters to Troy.

That was a mistake. She should have taken the time to truly understand her finances. That means reviewing reports regularly with Troy and questioning things that required clarification. She needed to spend time with Troy to communicate clearly what she needed and give him the tools he needed to succeed. By "getting around to finance," she set Troy up to fail and put her company in a much more precarious position than it needed to be.

In the early stages of a company's growth, founders rely on financial statements to make their decisions. Financial statements are standardized. They are the same format for every business. This enables investors and lenders to rely on consistent, understandable financial reports to evaluate funding opportunities. Financial statements are the reports every business uses to tell its financial story.

There are three of them:

1. **Profit and Loss:** Measures financial performance
2. **Balance Sheet:** A snapshot in time of your company's financial condition
3. **Statement of Cash Flows:** Shows how cash moves through your business

PROFIT AND LOSS

The Profit and Loss statement (P&L), also known as the Income Statement, measures financial performance by calculating Net Income. It appears at the bottom of the report, hence the term the "bottom line." The report is always presented in the same order regardless of the company, industry, or accountant.

It starts with revenue at the top, which includes all the money earned from the sale of goods and services. It's good practice to group your revenue into product categories so you can see which items drive the most sales in your business.

Below revenue is where we account for the cost of goods sold (called cost of revenue for service businesses). These costs include the direct costs of selling your product or service to a customer. This includes items like direct labor, product costs, shipping, application hosting costs, etc. The purpose of using direct costs is to give the owner a view on how much money is contributed solely by a sale to the customer. What's leftover covers overhead and profit.

Subtract cost of revenue from revenue and you get gross profit. This is a key performance indicator for your business that should be properly calculated, tracked, and measured. Investors and banks rely on gross profit to determine if they will fund your business. The number is benchmarked against your peers to see if the structural economics of your business are sound. If this amount is improperly calculated, or far below industry benchmarks, it will be questioned and may restrict your ability to raise funds on terms acceptable to you.

Operating expenses appear below cost of goods sold. Also known as indirect costs, these are expenses incurred running your business: sales and marketing, travel, office costs, facilities and compensation expenses not included in cost of goods sold. What is generally not included in this number is interest, taxes, depreciation or amortization. They are excluded to calculate EBITDA: Earnings Before Interest, Taxes, Depreciation & Amortization. This is a proxy for cash flow. It takes out certain non-operating costs that enable someone to better evaluate the core operational profitability of your business. If those costs are included in Operating Expenses, we refer to it as Operating Profit.

EBITDA is one of the most common terms you will hear when discussing the value of a company. It is why so many firms include it as a line item in their profit and loss statements. Since it focuses on core operations, it allows for a clearer comparison of financial performance without other expenses that could be considered variable. It removes non-cash expenses that don't directly impact cash flow and gives a more transparent view of cash without the interference of other financing and accounting policies.

Your company's Net Income is tallied by adjusting your EBITDA with other income and expenses like taxes, depreciation, interest, and extraordinary amounts.

Here are some takeaways about the Profit & Loss Statement:

1. It is a measure of financial performance, not cash flow. There are things that affect your cash on your balance sheet. Relying solely on the P&L for cash purposes will be misleading.

2. Gross profit and EBITDA will be heavily scrutinized by investors and lenders. If looking for capital or to exit, make sure yours are equal to or better than industry benchmarks when measured as a percentage of your net revenue.

3. A clean, understandable P&L not only provides you with greater clarity, it eases the preparation of financial projections.

BALANCE SHEET

The balance sheet is a snapshot of your company's financial position at a specific point in time. It has three sections: assets, liabilities, and equity. Within each section, items are listed in order of liquidity—the ease of which that item is converted into cash. The most liquid item, cash, is always at the top. If you took an accounting course at some point in your life, the one thing you probably remember from it is that assets must always equal liabilities plus equity.

1. Assets are what you OWN.
2. Liabilities are what you OWE.
3. Equity is what you are WORTH. This is what is left over when you subtract liabilities from assets.

Assets are what you own: cash, accounts receivable, inventory, etc. They are listed as current assets (those with a useful life twelve months or less), fixed (tangible assets with a useful life greater than twelve months), and noncurrent or other assets (intangible assets with a useful life greater than twelve months). Fixed assets are depreciated, and most noncurrent assets are amortized. Their value decreases over time to reflect their usage in the business.

Liabilities are what you owe: accounts payable, credit cards, loans, etc. Like assets, they are listed in the order in which they are due. Current liabilities are due in twelve months or less. Long-term liabilities are due longer than twelve months.

The final section of the balance sheet is Equity, which is what is leftover when you subtract liabilities from assets. It represents your stake in the business. Also called book value, it provides a starting point to understand your company's value. While it does not capture every aspect of market value or potential earnings, it is a useful metric for estimating what you are worth at a given point in time. However, the concept of equity on the balance sheet is often confusing for founders. To better illustrate this concept, think about it like purchasing a home.

- You buy a house (an asset) for $100,000.
- You take out a mortgage (liability) for $60,000.
- The $40,000 difference between the two is your equity.

Here are some takeaways about the balance sheet:

1. It is a snapshot in time—a statement of condition, not performance.
2. Banks rely on your balance sheet to determine if they will lend to you. Make sure they are properly prepared.
3. When projecting your company's cash flow, be sure to include the impact of balance sheet items like debt payments, receivables, and payables, as these will not be apparent on your profit and loss.

STATEMENT OF CASH FLOWS

The last statement Mike and Julien did not cover with Lindsey is probably the most obscure and the one that frustrates business owners the most. It is the Statement of Cash Flows. While it shows how cash moves in and out of the business, it will not answer questions like, *"How much cash did I spend on payroll last month?"* That's because its method of preparation, called the indirect method, is far easier than the direct method. Accounting software and public companies use the indirect method to calculate this financial statement.

It's interesting to note that this statement is created from data on the profit and loss statement and changes to amounts on the balance sheet. It contains no original data on its own. Its purpose is to show the changes to cash and the starting and ending balances for each period it is run.

There are three sections to it:

1. Cash flows from operating activities
2. Cash flows from investing activities
3. Cash flows from financing activities

At the bottom are the changes to cash flow, starting and ending cash balances.

Operating activities demonstrate the generation or utilization of cash in your core business activities: sales, expenses, and changes to the current sections of your balance sheet (collecting cash from receivables, paying off credit cards, etc.).

Investing activities are asset-related. When you purchase a fixed asset such as computers, equipment, or buildings, those purchases are shown as a reduction of cash.

Financing activities relate to how your business is capitalized. Raising debt, selling stock, contributions from partners and distributions to partners are all reflected here.

At the bottom of the statement of cash flow is a section showing whether the business generated or consumed cash. You'll also see your starting and ending cash balances for the period.

Here are some takeaways about the Statement of Cash Flows:

1. It is the least understood financial statement by founders because it is hard to understand and doesn't really tell us what we want to know.

2. It is the only financial statement focused on cash.

3. Understanding how cash moves through your company will provide great context. If you are running operating losses and must borrow money to cover your bills, the cash flow statement will show you how much cash you are long or short in each period.

Scan code to download sample financial statements
https://finforfounders.com/financial-statements

Scorecards, Charts, and Tables

For simplicity's sake, we won't go into all the scorecards, charts, and tables that Mike and Julien could have created for Lindsey. The growth in cloud apps has enabled a new generation of affordable, easy to use reporting tools that connect to accounting software like QuickBooks to provide financial reporting in a whole new way. They excel at transforming something that feels complex into something simpler that provides founders clear and actionable insights.

SCORECARD

A scorecard is designed to provide a quick snapshot of key performance indicators (KPIs). Business owners don't have time to sift through all the information in each of the various financial statements. A scorecard provides a reader with high priority metrics at a glance. Scorecards are ideal for highlighting goals and tracking performance against targets, such as revenue growth, profitability, or customer acquisition. A well-designed scorecard brings clarity by making essential information instantly accessible.

REVENUE (2025 YTD)

$3,862,976 ▲

+ $77,259 **vs budget**

Total Revenue for the year-to-date

Scorecard example

CHARTS

Charts are another great visual tool that can be created from accurate and well-organized financial statements. They help founders visualize trends, comparisons and changes over time. Different chart layouts can also convey information in easier to read formats.

Line and bar charts can be combined to relate two pieces of data. We can plot monthly revenue and rolling average revenue data to show how recent revenue trends impact the overall trajectory of revenue growth. There is no right or wrong way to create these charts. What is important is to communicate how you like to visualize your data, then have your financial team meet your requirement.

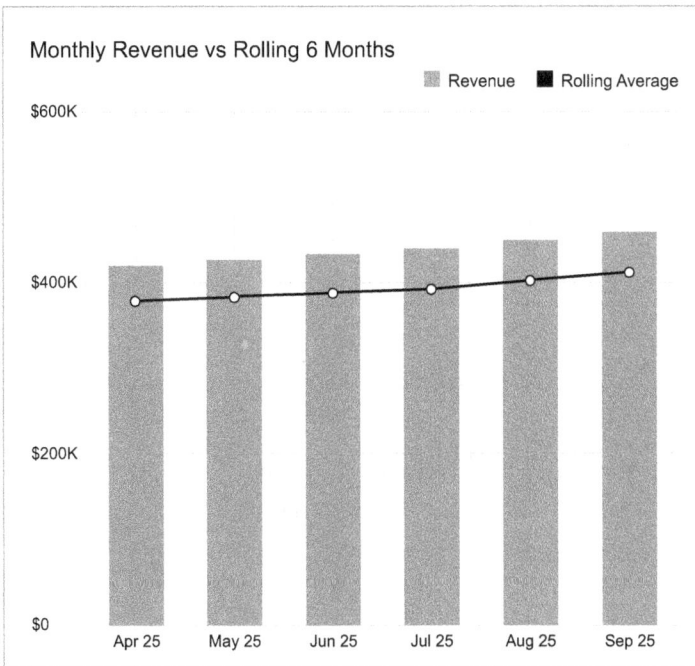

Monthly Revenue vs Rolling 6 Months

Revenue ▪ Rolling Average

Chart example

TABLES

Tables are not always as visually appealing as a chart or scorecard, but they serve a very distinct function breaking down financial data into detailed categories. Tables are best used when decision makers need to see exact figures or make specific comparisons. Examples of this could be analyzing sales by product line or operating expenses by type. By organizing data clearly, tables support deeper dives into specifics without overwhelming the reader.

KPI	Oct 2025	Sept 2025
Revenue	$129,666	$84,709
Operating Profit	$45,005	$3,848
Gross Profit	$75,456	$39,329
Net Income	$45,007	$3,849
Cash & Equivalents	$269,026	$227,434

Table example

The purpose of understanding different types of reports and visual aids is to show you the different ways available to display financial data. One of these options might be better than another depending on your need. To get to this point, the accounting data you use in your reporting must be solid. The most presentable charts are meaningless if the data used to create them is bad.

Monthly Financial Report

The monthly financial report is what ties all the other reporting together in a consolidated package. Instead of having to pull data from several different places, the report allows founders to easily conduct regular check-ups on the financial health of the company in a straightforward manner. The best reports have operational and financial information so the reader can see the financial impact of operations.

Monthly reports are most effective when reviewed during a standing monthly meeting. Typically, a senior financial executive will lead this discussion to help interpret the information. This meeting may be attended by members of the leadership team.

The structure of monthly reports can vary. Here's a format we've seen work well:

1. Executive summary
2. Separate sections reviewing revenue, profit, and cash
3. Operating metrics
4. Financial statements

Well-prepared reports contain explanatory notes to help the reader understand more complex items. The best ones are in a "drill-down" format. They begin with summarized data in the beginning, then contain sections that provide more detail. So, if you want to understand your accounts receivable scorecard, flip to an AR aging report later in the report to see who owes you and how old their invoices are since they were issued. If the report is issued online, this can be done through direct links or a table of contents, making navigation easy.

EXECUTIVE SUMMARY

The first section of the monthly report will contain an executive summary. If the reader reads nothing else, we want to communicate to them key information. This generally includes:

- A brief narrative
- Key topics for further discussion
- Scorecards for key revenue, cash, and profitability indicators
- High-level trend analysis

REVENUE, PROFIT AND CASH ANALYSIS

Separate sections for revenue, profit, and cash help the reader understand the performance drivers behind each of the Key Three objectives. These metrics are generally provided on a monthly and year-to-date basis. They include things like total revenue and growth rate, EBITDA, cash burn rate, total cash on hand, and partner distributions.

We usually provide charts outlining monthly trends, allowing the reader to detect patterns and adjust accordingly. The charts are also useful in showing progress against a target, as well as forecasting how that trend may continue.

OPERATING METRICS

Including certain operating metrics in the financial report is a great way to show the relationship between operating activities and financial performance.

Companies with recurring revenue like to track customer metrics such as Cost to Acquire a Customer and Lifetime Value of a Customer. Correlating trends in these metrics with financial metrics such as sales and EBITDA allows the reader to understand what operational activities are driving performance.

For example, if customer acquisition costs are too high, a founder can dive deeper into why that is happening. Is it taking too long to capture a new customer? Is the company overspending in an area that is not delivering sufficient return? You would not know how to ask these questions, nor know what an acceptable customer acquisition cost should be, if you were not measuring and evaluating it regularly.

FINANCIAL STATEMENTS

Within the financial report you will also be able to find the underlying financial statements discussed earlier in this chapter. These statements will usually be compiled with both month-to-date and year-to-date data. For example, the total revenue scorecard data will provide a sum of its individual line items on your P&L so you can see what makes up that number.

Comparing the numbers on these statements to the company's financial plan provides variances that can be improved with specific follow-up actions, holding your team accountable for improved financial performance. Going a step further and comparing the prior periods helps to set expectations around expected future performance.

Scan code to download a sample monthly report
https://finforfounders.com/monthly-report

Dashboards

When most people think of a dashboard they think of the one in their car. Everything they need to know about the overall health and safety of the vehicle is all in one place and updated in real time. Some of the indicators are going to be used more often than others. We're interested in the speedometer while travelling on the highway, we're not as interested in it when stopped at a traffic light.

Financial dashboards in your business are no different. They are a visual tool used to provide the reader with an at-a-glance view of their business's overall financial performance. They are meant to quickly inform.

Anyone without an accounting background should be able to understand the information in fifteen seconds or less. It should also be available on demand with the most current information possible. To achieve this, we always recommend using a cloud app and connecting it to other systems where it can pull in real time data. The cloud not only makes it interoperable, but your data will be available to you any time on any device connected to the internet.

There is no shortage of applications that will provide you with a dashboard. What is trickier is what to put on it. You can work with your team to decide what metrics would be most useful to have included on your company dashboard, but we always advise including data relevant to the Key Three Framework. Those metrics may include:

- YTD gross and net sales
- YTD EBITDA
- Cash on hand
- Open accounts receivable
- Open accounts payable
- Expenses by account
- Top customers listing by sales amount
- Top vendors by expense amount

ASSESSMENT: REPORTING

Rate yourself on the following questions according to how satisfied you are with each. Insert a number between one and ten in each box and add them up. One means you are very dissatisfied; ten means you are very satisfied:

1. How satisfied are you with the clarity and simplicity of your financial reports? _____

2. How easily can you customize your financial reports to focus on the specific metrics that matter most to your business? _____

3. How timely is the delivery of your financial reports? _____

4. How well do your financial reports help you understand the profitability of different parts of your business? _____

5. How satisfied are you with the financial dashboards or scorecards your company uses? _____

6. How satisfied are you with the ability of your financial reports to forecast future performance? _____

7. How aligned are your financial reports with industry benchmarks and KPIs? _____

8. How well do your financial reports integrate operational metrics (e.g., customer acquisition costs, lifetime value)? _____

9. How accessible and user-friendly are your financial reports for all stakeholders in your company? _____

10. How effective are your financial reports in helping you prepare for strategic discussions with investors, lenders, or partners? _____

Add up your score and write it here: _____

INTERPRETATION

Score Range: 10 to 60
At Risk

Your financial reporting is underperforming and could
be holding back your business. Consider significant investments
in your financial department to avoid costly mistakes
or missed opportunities.

Score Range: 61 to 80
Growth Opportunists

Your financial reporting is functional but has room for improvement.
Investing in better tools, training, or processes could unlock more
insights and efficiencies.

Score Range: 81 to 100
Confident Controllers

You have a strong financial reporting function. Keep refining your
processes to maintain your edge and adapt to growth.

Scan code to take the Reporting assessment online
https://finforfounders.com/reporting

6

Pillar 3:
Planning and Analysis

"**H**ey Lindsey," a soft voice said from the conference room door. "The food's here."

Lindsey looked up to see her assistant, Yvette, standing in front of a young delivery man holding two platters, one of baked goods and the other fruit. "Perfect," Lindsey said to Yvette then looked over her shoulder to the delivery man. "You can put everything on the table against the back wall." As he followed her instructions, Lindsey turned her attention back to Yvette. "Can you please let Troy know he can come in whenever he is ready?"

Yvette nodded and set forth for the task at hand. There were still ten minutes left before Mike and Julien were scheduled to arrive, but Lindsey wanted to make sure they were prepared to hit the ground running. It wasn't customary for Mike to block out half-day in-person working sessions. Given the progress they had made over the last ninety days and Lindsey's insistence on expediting their annual plan, he and Julien thought it would be good use of their time to tackle everything in one shot. The excitement and empowerment she felt from finally having a real grasp on her finances had her softly humming while taking the tops off the platters and getting lost in her own thoughts.

"You didn't need to spoil us like this," Mike joked as he entered the office with his laptop bag in hand and Julien a step behind him.

"Well, I was able to free up some budget for this special occasion," Lindsey joked while she shook Mike's free hand.

"That's what I like to hear!" Mike took his laptop out and placed it on the table in the center of the room as Lindsey shook hands with Julien. "Where would you like me to set up?"

"Anywhere you like. This will be very casual and collaborative," Lindsey said just as Troy appeared in the doorway with his laptop under one arm and a stack of papers in the other hand.

"Am I late?" Troy asked with genuine concern.

"Not at all," Lindsey smiled and motioned for him to sit down anywhere at the table.

It only took a few minutes for everyone to get settled in. Lindsey made it a point of standing in the center of everyone, but kept her attention focused mainly on Troy. "I want to thank you all for making the time to do this today. Troy, I'm sure it hasn't been easy to change the way you have always done things, and I want you to know how much I appreciate it. Do you have any questions before Mike and Julien kick us off with our annual planning for next year?"

Troy nearly blushed at the compliment as he leaned in closer to the table. "Nope. I'm just excited to see where this takes us next. My job has become much easier—and more interesting!"

"That's great news," Mike seized on the momentum. "Our annual plan is going to allow us to set realistic goals based on your objectives. We've come a long way from where we started. We want to continue that momentum by crafting a plan that brings us much higher profitability. With higher profits comes more cash, which will give Lindsey more options as she chooses how to put that cash to work.

"Let's begin with a high-level discussion on what you want to accomplish over the next few years," Mike said. "From that, we'll set some top-level objectives for the next year. These will be things like sales targets, any changes to services or distribution channels and hiring plans. When that's done we'll start building your plan, using your current chart of accounts to report the data. That way we can easily identify variances and come up with action items to improve them. Sound good?"

Everyone nodded their assent. Mike continued.

"Ultimately what we want to do is grow the valuation of your company. We'll have to keep in mind what people who may want to buy your company someday want to see. The two biggest drivers of value for companies in your life stage are sales growth and profitability—EBITDA. Our plan should seek to maximize these metrics. The good news is that if you are successful, you'll be generating ever increasing amounts of cash. Whether you choose to someday sell or not, you'll have the option to reinvest in the business and earn a great living."

Mike paused to let his last statement sink in a little. It was the first time he mentioned exiting in front of Troy. These conversations sometimes get a little tricky when someone other than the business owner is in the room.

Lindsey said, "Sounds like a sales forecast is going to be very important."

"It will be," replied Mike. "To do that we are going to start with your existing customer base and project how much business they will do with you next year. Ideally, we want to grow our wallet share with each of them. They already know, like, and trust you, so that is the low hanging fruit."

Lindsey made herself a quick note to have her client success team create a plan to contact existing clients and upsell them. "Easy enough. What else will we need?"

"We need to decide what key performance indicators are the most important. We need to forecast our cash flow for the year. All this needs to be done on a month-by-month basis." Mike looked from Lindsey to Troy to make sure they were both still following along with him. "From there we can decide what additional metrics you should track and measure. Then we have to get that data to track and measure them."

It was going to be a lot of work. But if they were successful, the rewards could be huge.

"I think it's time for a bagel," Lindsey said jokingly, eager to get going on her first roadmap to a brighter financial future.

* * *

Lindsey and Troy were completely bought-in to the process Mike and Julien implemented. The accurate, timely data from her accounting activities informed new reports that provided insights she never had before. The speed at which she could get the data—and answers to any of her questions—was remarkable to her.

The additional time she now had from not working so hard to get financial information was noticeable. She can now focus on higher level activities worthy of her time, such as planning for the future. When she was working so hard just to get good data, Lindsey could not focus on effective financial planning and analysis (referred to as FP&A), which would drive up the value of her business.

By setting financial goals aligned with a solid growth strategy, founders ensure their business decisions support long-term objectives. Short term goals are valuable only when they support the longer-term vision. Most business owners are so busy that they lack the time to find the quiet space to just plan. Upgrading your financial system can provide you that time and data to plan effectively.

Mike and Julien spent the rest of the working session taking Lindsey and Troy through other important aspects of planning and analysis. The plan will create Key Performance Indicators (KPIs) to ensure they are always focused on continuously improving their sales, profit, and cash flow. The timeframe for the plan is monthly; it is reviewed, delivered and updated each month.

For companies that may be concerned with cash flow, a more tactical approach is the weekly cash flow forecast. This is different from an annual plan. It is planning for how your company will manage cash flow each week looking ahead for the next three months.

While it informs the annual plan, the cash flow forecast's purpose is quite different. Its purpose is to make sure enough cash is generated to pay the bills.

Financial ratios are KPIs typically used by external people to evaluate a company for lending, investing, or purchasing. We'll introduce some financial ratios and how to utilize them in a way that is not too complex, abstract, or challenging to interpret.

Finally, we'll introduce some common financial analyses we have found to make the biggest impact for founders in gaining better control of their overall financial situation.

Annual Financial Plan

The annual plan is the roadmap the company will follow each month for the next twelve months. We start working on them in the fourth quarter of the prior year, then finalize after closing the last month of the year so we have good starting balances.

The planning process itself is where you'll get the most value from your plan. It will help you think through what's important and help you prioritize what needs to get done in the coming year.

Plans are dynamic. You'll be planning throughout the year as you adapt to changing business conditions. If your efforts are exceeding expectations in an area, then continue those efforts. If not, choose areas to scale back so you can achieve your sales, cash, and profit objectives. Schedule a standing meeting each month to assess where you are at that moment in time and update your forecast. You should "roll" the forecasts to add additional months, so you always have a forward twelve-month view of your business.

> **FINSIGHT**
>
> **The value of a plan is in the planning, not the plan itself.**

GETTING STARTED

The first step is to set your overall goals for sales, profitability, and cash flow. Whatever you want to see happen in the next twelve months should align with the longer-term strategic plan, covering the next three to five years. Set the annual targets first. You can work backward to fill in the months and other details.

Start with your profit and loss statement. Forecast amounts by the accounts from your chart of accounts. If you followed the advice in Chapter 4, you should have a clean chart to work with. Begin with revenue and cost of revenue so you can see what your projected gross profit will be.

From there, collect data on the major categories of operating expenses—compensation and benefits, as well as sales and marketing. Get a handle on what percentage of revenue you'll invest in these key areas because they are your primary drivers of growth. If you need a reference, get benchmark data from the P&Ls of public companies like yours, or ask your favorite AI app. After that, model any product development costs and other overhead.

WHAT TO MODEL ON YOUR P&L

As we continue the planning process it will be important to enter projections of target spending in four key areas:

1. Revenue, preferably broken down by product line
2. Cost of revenue (cost of goods sold), to get gross profit
3. Major expenses: labor costs, sales and marketing, product development
4. All other expenses

Founders that do not have formal sales forecasts struggle with forecasting revenue, especially if they have never done it before. The easiest thing to do is look at what you have done historically and increase it by a certain percentage each month from the prior year. If you have achieved that target you are guaranteed to grow your sales.

If scale is what you seek, set your target annual percentage increase slightly larger than what you did the year before.

The cost of goods sold is a variable cost—it fluctuates with how much you sell. You can enter a simple percentage of sales if it's been consistent over time. If you have good data, model in other components like labor cost, subcontractors, product costs, etc. Reduce that percentage slightly during the year so you can show improvement in your gross profit. Of course, if you plan to reduce your cost of sales be sure to implement initiatives that will actually reduce those costs.

The biggest spending category for a company is the cost of its people. Invest a good chunk of your planning time in your labor plan. Develop a census of employees and calculate their salaries, incentive comp, and any raises for the year. Add in any potential new hires. Don't forget to model other costs, such as payroll taxes, benefits, and recruiting. When you've developed this census, you can calculate your total monthly amounts and transfer them to your plan. The cost of compensation and benefits is consistent as a percentage of revenue in an industry. Validate these costs by benchmarking your compensation percentage of net revenue to your peers.

Growth companies must spend their sales and marketing dollars wisely to efficiently grow revenue. Develop your sales and marketing plans, then cost them by your spending categories on your chart of accounts. This will help you measure the return on your marketing investment.

For example, if digital advertising is effectively driving qualified leads, you may want to increase your ad spending and creative fees but reduce spending on events to get the results you want. If you pay sales commissions, book them here, not in the cost of goods sold. If you've heard the term "Selling, General, and Administrative Expenses," then you'll see that any selling costs are operating expenses.

Finally, model the rest of your spending with increases less than your revenue increase. This ensures that each dollar of new revenue adds more profit to your company. A couple of focus areas are IT spending and new product development. It is always enlightening to realize how many subscriptions many companies have that they no longer use or don't even realize they are paying for in the first place. Review your subscriptions and eliminate those no longer needed. Many companies outsource their new product development, and the cost of external resources can quickly grow large. See if any outsourced services could be brought in-house at lower cost.

MODELING YOUR BALANCE SHEET

Now that your P&L is effectively drafted, the next step is looking at your balance sheet to see the impact on your cash position. Remember, your P&L is not indicative of cash flow and cannot be used as a stand-alone document for cash forecasting. You must develop a balance sheet and then make assumptions based on that data to assess that impact. This gets tricky for founders doing their own modeling since it requires some accounting knowledge to get it done right.

Whether you choose to do it yourself or not, you should know what can be modeled so you understand its impact on your cash. How you create the balance sheet is not necessarily important, but the items you track on it will be. Numerous items can be modeled to optimize cashflow using financial ratios that we get to later in this chapter. The items with the most potential for impacting your cash flow are:

- Accounts receivable
- Inventory
- Accounts payable
- Deferred revenue
- Debt service
- Owner distributions

Since a balance sheet is a snapshot in time, you model running balances instead of transaction amounts like those on a P&L. For example, if your sales go up, your receivables go up. We can track receivables using a day's sales outstanding metric that ties to how long it takes to collect cash from your customers. If you want to collect payments quicker, model a lower day's sales outstanding accounts receivable metric and back it up with a program to encourage faster payments. You can see how balance sheet modeling can get complex. It is highly useful, however, to project your cash balances throughout the year.

Many founders begin wondering just how much cash is considered enough cash to have on hand and be comfortable. Everyone has a different tolerance for decreasing bank balances, but we have found two metrics that tend to satisfy most.

The first is having the equivalent of ten percent of annual sales in the bank at any point in time. So, if you have a million dollars annual revenue, $100,000 is a safe cash balance. The other option would be an amount equivalent to three months of cash burn rate.

FINSIGHT

Keep ten percent of your annual revenue or three months burn rate cash on hand. Cash on hand can include availability on your line of credit.

If you find your cash flow is not where you'd like it to be, you have some options. First is to lower your spending to increase operating cash flow. Next is to seek out external funding through increases in your line of credit or equity financing. We encourage founders to open a line of credit at the start of their business, even if it's not needed. Finally, as the owner you could elect to take lower distributions from the company to fund its growth. Each one of these options has tradeoffs you should consider carefully as you prepare to invest in next year's growth.

At this point, your annual financial plan is effectively done. Create a document to memorialize it. If you use a budgeting app, load the plan into it. Each month, run a budget versus actual report and review variances with a focus on examining and correcting any performance below a certain threshold.

MAINTAINING THE PLAN

You should have a standing monthly meeting with your team and/or a financial advisor to review performance and update the forward plan. Some companies perform cursory monthly reviews and more detailed quarterly ones. The important thing is that you must activate your plan to make it effective. It must become part of your regular workflow. It can't be emailed and left in an inbox. Just as you would not turn off your GPS until you arrive at your destination, you can't turn off your plan.

When you update the plan during the year, save it as a new one titled your "Latest Estimate." As the year progresses, your annual plan gets stale, and your latest estimate becomes more valuable as an indicator of how your year will end. The "Latest Estimate" will be the guiding document. Near the end of the year the time will come to start crafting the annual financial plan for the next fiscal year.

Scan code to download a sample financial plan
https://finforfounders.com/financial-plan

Key Performance Indicators (KPIs)

The term key performance indicator is so commonly used in business that there are times it feels like it can be applied to anything. Let's narrow it down to the KPIs that are important to founders.

We split these indicators into the categories of financial and operational. The financial KPIs come from your financial data. They show the financial impact of your operations. Operational KPIs help you execute better. These are metrics you track to do things more efficiently, like generate leads, close deals, or improve customer satisfaction.

An example is revenue and billable hours. Revenue is a financial metric resulting from billing your people's time to a client. Billable hours are used for billing time and the type of time, so you charge the correct hourly rate. It's also used to staff jobs to make sure you have the right people doing the right work. Billable hours are an operating KPI that drives the revenue financial KPI.

Many financial KPIs will come out of your financial plan and can be grouped into categories aligned with the Key Three objectives. In the sales category we recommend:

- Total revenue
- Revenue by product line
- Revenue growth
- Sales reductions, such as refunds or returns

Profitability KPIs typically include:

- Gross profit
- Gross profit percentage of revenue
- EBITDA
- EBITDA percentage of revenue
- Profit by customer or project

Cash KPIs include:

- Total cash on hand
- Changes to cash
- Operating cash flow

Operational KPIs vary based on your business model. There are some that are more relevant to recurring revenue models and others that are for tangible products. Here is a list of some common ones you may have heard of:

- Cost to acquire a customer
- Lifetime value of a customer
- Churn rate
- Monthly recurring revenue
- Unit volume
- Number of active customers
- Revenue per employee
- Billable hours
- Utilization percentage

Scan code to download a list of common KPIs
https://finforfounders.com/kpis

We want our KPIs to be relevant. Each one is something that we can control. We then want to know its current measure and whether it is favorable or unfavorable to where we want that metric to be.

For example, in a recurring revenue business we want our lifetime value of a customer to be at least three times the cost to acquire a customer. This is a common benchmark for any sustainable business. If we compute this KPI and learn that is not the case, then the business is structurally unsustainable: it is not generating enough cash flow from its operations. Without changes, eventually the business will not be able to generate enough cash to fund itself. If you were the owner of this company you'd ask your team some questions:

1. Can I increase pricing or gross profit margins to improve the lifetime value of a customer?
2. Which marketing programs need to be reevaluated to lower cost and thus my cost to acquire a customer?
3. Are customers leaving us so quickly that we haven't had a chance to recoup our investment?

Each one of these questions requires further analysis and perhaps some changes to strategy to make the business model more sustainable. This is where the right KPIs can be very powerful for your business. You would not think about examining these areas unless you had the data to do so. It's like the classic quote attributed to Peter Drucker: *"What gets measured gets done."*

Key performance indicators can be leading indicators or lagging indicators. Leading KPIs are used to predict future performance, either financially or operationally. A good example of this would be a sales pipeline and how the steps involved in the process build on one another. Each step can be tracked and measured to give you an indication of what your sales are going to be:

1. Capture a lead (Marketing Qualified Lead or MQL)
2. Qualify a lead as a prospect (Sales Qualified Lead or SQL)
3. Meet with the prospect
4. Send them a quote or proposal
5. Capture if the proposal was accepted or rejected

In order to win new work, we have to meet with the prospect and issue them a proposal. We can track these leading indicators to help us forecast sales:

1. Number of SQLs
2. Number of initial meetings
3. Number of proposals delivered
4. Conversion percentage of accepted proposals to total proposals delivered
5. Average value of an accepted proposal

With greater clarity on our sales pipeline, we can develop a more meaningful revenue forecast. We can track and measure the leading indicators and their resulting revenue all in one place. This helps us more easily detect patterns and spot what is working for us.

Lagging KPIs are used to reflect past performance. Revenue is a lagging indicator of a sale that has been made, and the purchase has been delivered. These metrics are far more abundant than leading KPIs because this data is readily available from invoices to your customers. There is no way to know if what you have been doing over the last month, quarter, or year is working unless you have benchmarks for success to evaluate the current strategies. In addition to sales, some commonly used lagging indicators are gross and net profit margin, accounts receivable aging, and customer retention rate.

Using the above example, the lagging sales indicator is built upon the leading indicators in your sales funnel. By measuring both you get clear, direct insight into what is driving your sales. *Do you need more meetings? A higher conversion rate?* The data will tell you your most efficient path to a robust sales pipeline and continuously higher revenue.

You can create targets for your KPIs just like you forecast your P&L. When we measure their performance, we get great insights to what will happen next. If you get negative variances in your leading indicators you are going to know ahead of time that your sales may drop off in a quarter or two. *What would you do with that information now if you knew what was going to happen later?* That's the power of tracking KPIs.

If you struggle finding suitable KPIs for your business, just ask around. Speak with others in your industry, fellow business owners, or accountants. A quick internet search will turn up lots of answers. Don't develop too many KPIs at first. Keep it to less than ten and focus on a few at a time until you develop a sense for what works for you.

While this sounds like a lot to manage, your time and effort will be well rewarded. Once there is a well-organized system in place for compiling and tracking the data, you only need an hour or so a month to continuously monitor improvement. Start by improving high-priority negative variances to make incremental progress. No one expects immediate massive gains. Regular, small gains can add up quickly after a quarter or two.

KPIs Summary

Financial KPIs	**Operational KPIs**
• Revenue	• Cost to acquire a customer
• Cash on hand	• Revenue per employee
• EBITDA	• Billable hours
Leading Indicators	**Lagging Indicators**
• Number of new leads	• Revenue
• Number of prospect meetings	• Accounts receivable
• Proposals won	• EBITDA

Cash Flow Forecasting

Cash flow forecasting is one of the most practical tools in a founder's financial toolbox, and it's distinct from the broader annual plan. While an annual plan provides a high-level roadmap for where the business is headed over the next year, a cash flow forecast focuses on the here and now. It's about ensuring your company has liquidity to cover its bills, payroll, and other immediate obligations. This tactical focus can be the difference between smooth operations and a cash crunch that disrupts your business.

> **FINSIGHT**
>
> **A cash flow forecast ensures there's enough cash in the bank to navigate the next three months. It is prepared weekly.**

A typical cash flow forecast is prepared each week for the following thirteen weeks on a rolling basis. Finish one week, then add another. This weekly approach gives founders a detailed view of their immediate financial future, highlighting potential shortfalls or surpluses. It's like using binoculars instead of a telescope—you're not planning for next year's growth initiatives; you're ensuring that there's enough cash in the bank to navigate the next three months. Some founders start with weekly cash flow meetings, then move to bi-monthly or monthly as they get a handle on cash flow.

Building a cash flow forecast starts with gathering data. Name who you owe—vendors, suppliers, employees—and map out when payments are due. Then layer in your expected inflows, such as customer payments or other revenue streams. This exercise models your cash flow week by week, creating a clear picture of how money moves in and out of your business. With this information in hand, you can make informed decisions about which bills to prioritize, when to negotiate terms, and whether additional financing is needed.

The good news is that cash flow forecasting doesn't require expensive software. Many founders start with a simple Excel spreadsheet. Rows are names of customers and vendors, columns are weeks. Put your data in and move the amounts around so you can see your weekly changes to cash and starting and ending cash balances.

Alternatively, there are apps designed specifically for cash flow management that can automate data collection and analysis, saving time and reducing errors. Many of them plug into your accounting software, automating data retrieval.

The key is consistency; whether it's Excel or an app, the forecast needs to be updated regularly to remain useful. It can be time-consuming, so it's best to know yourself well enough to know when to get some help. It's a critical activity worth spending some money on, even during times when cash is tight. The investment often quickly pays for itself.

If there are periods where cash flow threatens to go negative, you will have the foresight to make adjustments that lessen its impact. That could include asking certain vendors to change due dates to coincide with when your customers pay you or adjusting the invoicing to your clients, so their payments coincide with the time of month when you are most in need of the positive cash flow.

When done right, a cash flow forecast gives founders peace of mind. You may not like what you see, but you will be prepared, and removing that uncertainty removes a lot of stress. You'll know exactly who to pay and when, eliminating guesswork and avoiding the stress of scrambling for cash. It's a straightforward yet powerful way to stay on top of your finances and keep your business moving forward.

Scan code to download a sample cash flow forecast
https://finforfounders.com/cash-flow-forecast

Using Financial Ratios

Using financial ratios can be confusing for many founders because there is often no context to help evaluate them. The context we use is our peer group—companies like ours. If we can learn the ratios of high performers in our industry; we can model our metrics to mimic the same performance.

Let's use personal health as our framework for evaluating financial ratios for our business. When we go to the doctor, they will perform tests on our blood pressure, glucose levels, and other measurements of our physical health. Those are expressed as ratios, then compared to a benchmark.

Some ratios may be more important. If there is a history of high cholesterol in our family, for example, we may pay more attention to that and other cardiac indicators. We filter out indicators that are not as meaningful for us so we can focus on those that are. But we also need to include enough indicators because things change over time. We measure things that may not be important now in order to gain visibility of a future problem.

Just as your doctor will tell you whether you are healthy or not based on the results of a check-up, investors and lenders will be very candid about what they think of the financial health of your company. The ratios they evaluate line up with the Key Three objectives: sales, profit, and cash.

People looking to fund your business are most concerned with profitability. The ongoing sustainability of a business is measured by its ability to generate internal cash flow. Those that are highly profitable will not have problems raising funds. The opposite is also true. There are some lenders who will not lend to a company with negative EBITDA—it's too much risk for them.

What if we are not actively looking to raise capital? Ratios are very useful in running our business. There are operating ratios that founders use all the time and may not know it. Let's first review some ratios important for founders to understand when it comes to making daily operational decisions. Then we'll evaluate ratios useful to banks and investors. Below are just a handful of many financial ratios available.

PROFITABILITY RATIOS

These ratios measure financial performance.

Gross Profit Margin as a Percentage of Revenue

$$\text{Gross Profit Margin \%} = \left(\frac{\text{Gross Profit}}{\text{Net Revenue}} \right) \times 100$$

Where:

- **Gross Profit** = Net Revenue minus Cost of Goods Sold (COGS)
- **Net Revenue** = Total revenue minus any returns, allowances, or discounts

Gross profit margin is one of the key financial ratios founders should be concerned with when it comes to overall profitability. This ratio shows the percentage of revenue remaining after covering the direct costs of producing goods or services. A healthy gross profit margin indicates the company can cover production costs with enough left over to fund operations, growth and payments to the founder. It's particularly useful for tracking cost efficiency and pricing strategies.

EBITDA as a Percentage of Revenue

As discussed, EBITDA stands for Earnings Before Interest, Taxes, Depreciation and Amortization. Its formula is:

$$\text{EBITDA \% of Net Revenue} = \left(\frac{\text{EBITDA}}{\text{Net Revenue}} \right) \times 100$$

EBITDA is calculated one of two ways:

EBITDA = Net Income + Interest + Taxes + Depreciation + Amortization

– OR –

Gross Profit Margin – Operating Expenses

Where:

- **Net Income** is the company's profit after all expenses.
- **Interest** refers to the cost of borrowing funds or income earned on cash balances.
- **Taxes** include deductible taxes paid or owed. Deductibility of taxes depends on how you are incorporated and jurisdictions where your company is subject to taxes on its operations.
- **Depreciation** accounts for the reduction in value of tangible assets over time.
- **Amortization** represents the gradual write-off of intangible assets.

EBITDA percentage measures the percentage of revenue left after deducting all operating expenses except taxes, interest, depreciation, and amortization. By excluding one-time and non-operating expenses, it shows the company's ability to generate cash.

It is a key metric used by company buyers when setting a valuation of a company. Most offers to purchase a company are calculated as a multiple of EBITDA.

Net Profit Margin

Finally, we have Net Profit Margin, which reveals the portion of revenue that remains as profit after all other income and expenses are deducted. This is your taxable income if you are incorporated as a pass-through entity.

$$Net\ Profit\ Margin\ \% = \left(\frac{Net\ Profit}{Net\ Revenue} \right) \times 100$$

It measures how effectively your company is converting revenue into actual profit. This is your bottom-line profitability and can be compared to your peer group to see if your profits are above or below the benchmark.

LIQUIDITY RATIOS

The next set of ratios important to founders are liquidity ratios. This measures your company's ability to generate and keep enough cash on hand to fund operations.

Current Ratio

The Current Ratio measures a company's ability to cover its short-term liabilities with its short-term assets. A ratio above 1.0 generally indicates good liquidity, which is vital for founders to ensure their business can meet its immediate financial obligations without running into cash flow issues.

$$\text{Current Ratio} = \frac{\text{Current Assets}}{\text{Current Liabilities}}$$

Where:

- **Current Assets:** Assets expected to be converted into cash or used within one year (e.g., cash, accounts receivable, inventory)
- **Current Liabilities:** Obligations due within one year (e.g., accounts payable, short-term debt, accrued expenses)

Note that you can quickly determine your company's working capital amount from the inputs to this formula. It is simply current assets minus current liabilities, which are amounts you can find on your most recent balance sheet. Positive working capital indicates the company can meet its short-term obligations and still invest in growth, while negative working capital may signal cash flow challenges and put the company in a position where cash could run out soon.

Days Sales Outstanding

Days Sales Outstanding (DSO) tracks the number of days on average it takes a company to collect payment after a sale. It's useful for monitoring cash flow and evaluating the efficiency of your accounts receivable process.

$$DSO = \left(\frac{Account\ Receivable}{Total\ Credit\ Sales} \right) \times Number\ of\ Days$$

Where:

- **Accounts Receivable:** The amount owed to the company by customers for goods or services sold on credit
- **Total Credit Sales:** Revenue generated from sales made on credit (those with an open invoice amount) during the same period
- **Number of Days:** The time frame for which the DSO is being calculated (e.g., thirty days for a month, 365 days for a year)

Most companies strive for DSO that is thirty days or less. Typical collection patterns in your industry or who you sell to matters. Selling to healthcare providers, for example, may result in a much higher DSO.

Investors and banks will evaluate the profitability and liquidity ratios we just mentioned. They will also focus on ratios that assess risk. *How confident are they that they will get paid back with a sufficient return to compensate the risk they took?*

It helps to understand the risk profiles of an investor versus a lender. A lender wants assurance you will pay back the money loaned to you with interest. They'll demand guarantees and collateral so they have recourse (as an alternative means to collect) if you can't repay the loan as specified in the terms of your loan agreement.

Investors have no such guarantees. They are concerned with receiving a suitable rate of return for any money they provide. Since they are not getting a repayment guarantee they have higher risk, thus demand a higher return as compensation.

These are some of the ratios that lenders and investors will evaluate:

Debt-to-Equity Ratio

Debt-to-equity is one of the first ratios both banks and investors want to see. This ratio indicates the relative proportion of debt and equity used to finance a company's assets.

$$\text{Debt to Equity Ratio} = \frac{\text{Total Liabilities}}{\text{Total Shareholder's Equity}}$$

Where:

- **Total Liabilities:** Includes all debts and obligations the company owes (e.g., accounts payable, accrued expenses, lines of credit)
- **Total Shareholders' Equity:** Represents the owners' residual interest in the company after liabilities are deducted from assets

Lenders use this ratio to assess risk of you repaying back your loan. A high debt-to-equity ratio requires more cash to service existing debt, presenting more risk to the lender. An investor may think they need to put more cash in the business if total outstanding debt does not improve. Debt isn't a bad thing, but lopsided proportions when compared to equity can quickly become a red flag.

Return on Equity

$$\text{Return on Equity} = \left(\frac{\text{Net Income}}{\text{Shareholder's Equity}} \right) \times 100$$

Where:

- **Net Income:** The company's total earnings after all expenses have been deducted
- **Shareholders' Equity:** The residual value of assets minus liabilities, representing the owners' investment in the company

Return on Equity measures how effectively a company generates profit from its shareholders' investments. A higher ROE is attractive to investors, as it indicates the company is generating strong returns on the equity invested by shareholders, signaling effective management and potential for growth. Just like a well-performing stock in the market, investors are more likely to go where they can comfortably expect returns that align with their overall investment strategy.

Operating Cash Flow Ratio

$$\text{Operating Cash Flow Ratio} = \frac{\text{Operating Cash Flow}}{\text{Current Liabilities}}$$

Where:

- **Operating Cash Flow:** The cash generated from a company's normal business operations, found on the cash flow statement
- **Current Liabilities:** Short-term obligations that are due within a year, such as accounts payable, accrued expenses, and short-term debt

Operating Cash Flow Ratio is a ratio that examines how well the company can cover its current liabilities from cash generated by core operations. Since it reflects the ability to generate cash from regular business activities, it is valuable for lenders who are concerned with cash flow sustainability for debt repayment.

The key component of this ratio is the focus on "core" operations. Investors are not concerned with one-time events like the sale of an asset for cash. They want to see that day-to-day business operations are enough to sustain the company.

Debt Service Ratio

$$Debt\ Service\ Ratio = \frac{Net\ Operating\ Income}{Total\ Debt\ Service}$$

Where:

- **Net Operating Income (NOI):** Income generated from the company's operations, typically calculated as revenue minus operating expenses
- **Total Debt Service:** The sum of all principal and interest payments on the company's debts over a given period

The Debt Service Ratio is also known as the Debt Service Coverage Ratio (DSCR). It measures a company's ability to meet its debt obligations with its operating income. A ratio greater than 1.0 indicates that the company generates sufficient income to cover its debt payments, while a ratio below 1.0 signals potential difficulties in meeting obligations. Lenders view a high DSCR as a strong indicator of creditworthiness, while investors may see it as a sign of stable cash flow, enhancing confidence in the company's ability to manage debt responsibly while growing.

When it comes to financial ratios, start with ones that are easy to understand and are directly tied to your business goals. If you plan to seek capital, ask lenders and investors what ratios they are currently evaluating. Calculate those and see if they are within the benchmarks where the market is comfortable funding a company like yours.

Scan code to download financial ratios
https://finforfounders.com/ratios

Five Common Financial Analysis Examples

Financial analysis might sound intimidating, but it's one of the most powerful tools for founders to make informed decisions that drive growth.

While there are countless types of analyses available, this section focuses on five that are straightforward, effective, and commonly prepared by CFOs of growing companies:

1. Pricing
2. Trend
3. Unit economics
4. Cost
5. Breakeven

Each provides actionable insights into key areas of your business, helping you make smarter choices to achieve higher sales, profits, and cash flow. By mastering your understanding of these foundational analyses, you'll gain a clearer view of your company's financial health and future potential.

PRICING ANALYSIS

Pricing analysis involves determining the optimal price point for products and services to ensure both profitability and competitiveness in the marketplace. We look at them three ways:

1. Cost-Plus Pricing
2. Competitive Analysis
3. Value-Based Pricing

Each method can stand on its own. They are more effective when each is performed and their insights are combined so you have the data to determine your most effective pricing strategy.

Cost Plus Pricing

Cost-Plus Pricing calculates the total cost of producing a product or service, then adding a specific mark-up to ensure profitability.

Why It's Useful:

- Provides a straightforward way to ensure costs are covered while generating profit
- Reduces complexity by focusing only on internal costs and desired margins

Best Situations:

- Ideal for businesses with stable production costs and minimal market fluctuations
- Works well when introducing a new product with minimal competitive data available
- Best suited for industries where price transparency and cost justification are critical, such as manufacturing or professional services

Drawbacks:

- This method doesn't account for competitors' pricing or customer perceptions, which could result in prices that are too high or too low for the market.
- If production costs are high, prices may exceed what customers are willing to pay. Conversely, low costs might lead to missed opportunities for higher margins.
- It emphasizes internal cost structures rather than external factors like market demand or value to the customer.

Competitive Analysis

Competitive Analysis compares your prices with both competitor products and substitute products to gain a better understanding of market positioning and customer perceptions.

Why It's Useful:

- Helps position your product or service in the marketplace relative to competitors
- Ensures your pricing reflects market expectations, reducing the risk of being overpriced or undervalued

Best Situations:

- Particularly useful in highly competitive markets where pricing is a key differentiator
- Works well for businesses entering a new market and seeking to establish a competitive foothold
- Essential for industries like retail or SaaS where customer perception of value is closely tied to pricing relative to competitors

Drawbacks:

- Too much focus on competitors' pricing can lead to neglecting unique value propositions or internal cost structures.
- Matching competitors' prices doesn't guarantee that the price covers your costs or aligns with your financial goals.
- Customers may value unique features or services that aren't reflected in competitors' prices.

Value-Based Pricing

The third method is Value-Based Pricing, which is where prices are set based on the perceived value to customers rather than solely on costs. To effectively utilize this method, you must first research customer needs and determine how much they would be willing to pay.

Why It's Useful:

- Maximizes revenue potential by aligning pricing with what customers are willing to pay
- Focuses on customer satisfaction and perceived value, fostering loyalty and repeat business

Best Situations:

- Effective for premium products or services with unique features or strong brand equity
- Works well in industries where innovation or exclusivity drives demand, such as technology, luxury goods, or consulting
- Suitable for businesses offering solutions that significantly impact customer success, allowing for higher pricing justified by ROI

Drawbacks:

- Requires in-depth market research to understand customer needs and willingness to pay, which can be time-consuming and costly
- If perceived value is overestimated, prices may alienate customers. Underestimating value could leave money on the table
- This method often demands ongoing engagement with customers and data analysis to keep pricing aligned with perceived value

Pricing Examples

A software company is evaluating options to set the the monthly price of its subscription.

Cost-Plus Pricing:

- Development, hosting, and support costs are $20 per user per month. Applying a fifty percent markup, the price is set at $30.

Competitive Analysis:

- Competitors charge between $25 and $35. The company positions itself in the middle at $30, offering additional features to justify the higher range.

Value-Based Pricing:

- Customers report that the app saves them $100 per month in manual work. Based on this value, the company tests pricing at $40, capturing higher perceived value.

A significant benefit from pricing analysis, no matter which method you use, is optimizing profit margins. By choosing the right pricing method for the right situation, you can set prices strategically to achieve your goals, whether it's ensuring profitability, competing effectively, or capturing the maximum value from customers.

Scan code to download a sample pricing analysis
https://finforfounders.com/pricing-analysis

UNIT ECONOMICS

Unit Economics focuses on understanding the profitability of a single unit of product or service. By analyzing how much profit one unit generates, you can gain valuable insights into your business's operational efficiency, pricing strategy, and scalability. This analysis is particularly critical for identifying what's driving profitability—or holding it back.

Why It's Useful:

- Clarifies the scalability of your business model by showing whether profitability improves with increased sales volume
- Identifies cost drivers to highlight areas for efficiency improvements
- Validates pricing strategies by directly linking changes to the contribution margin and ensuring sustainable profit margins

Best Situations:

- Essential for subscription or product-based businesses looking to scale operations efficiently
- Ideal for evaluating the feasibility of launching a new product or service
- Valuable when facing rising costs or competitive pressure to ensure margins remain intact

How to Perform Unit Economics Analysis:

1. **Calculate Revenue Per Unit:** This is the price at which a single unit is sold. It forms the starting point for evaluating the profitability of each unit.
2. **Account for Direct Costs:** Include all costs directly related to producing and delivering the unit, such as labor, materials, shipping, and commissions.

3. **Determine the Contribution Margin:** It subtracts direct costs from revenue per unit. The Contribution Margin represents what's left to cover overhead and contribute to net profit.

Unit Economics example:

Let's evaluate a digital marketing consultancy offering pay-per-click (PPC) campaign services. Each project generates $5,000 in revenue. Direct costs include $1,000 for ad spend, $800 for freelancer fees, and $200 for software tools, totaling $2,000.

The contribution margin for each project is $3,000 ($5,000 minus $2,000), which covers overhead like office space and salaries while leaving room for profit. By improving operational efficiency, such as automating reporting, the consultancy can reduce freelancer costs and boost the contribution margin to $3,200 per project, improving overall profitability.

Scan code to download a sample unit economics analysis
https://finforfounders.com/unit-economics

TREND ANALYSIS

Trend Analysis involves examining historical data to identify patterns, trends, and changes over time. This analysis helps businesses understand how key factors—such as sales, expenses, and market conditions—are evolving, providing a strong foundation for forecasting and strategic decision-making. By spotting potential issues early, businesses can proactively address challenges before they escalate.

Why It's Useful:

- Reveals patterns that inform better decision-making and long-term planning
- Highlights areas of concern or opportunity, enabling timely interventions
- Supports effective resource allocation by identifying where investments will yield the highest returns

Best Situations:

- Ideal for evaluating the success of sales and marketing initiatives over time
- Essential for monitoring financial health during periods of growth or market fluctuation
- Valuable for predicting future cash flow needs and avoiding shortfalls

How to Perform Trend Analysis:

1. **Focus on the Key Three Objectives:**
   - Analyze seasonality and growth patterns to fund investments and evaluate the effectiveness of sales and marketing efforts.
   - Track metrics like gross and net profit margins to monitor financial health and identify potential issues.

- Assess liquidity, monthly cash burn, and operating cash flow to ensure the business can meet its obligations.

2. **Use Visualization Techniques:**

   - Plot data on line graphs and bar charts to make patterns and trends easier to understand.
   - Apply moving averages to smooth out short-term fluctuations and highlight longer-term trends.
   - Calculate percentage changes over specific time periods to quantify shifts and their impact.

3. **Analyze and Act:**

   - Look for consistent upward or downward trends and assess their causes.
   - Use insights to refine strategies, allocate resources, and make data-driven decisions.

Trend Analysis example:

A boutique e-commerce store notices that its sales spike every November and December but dip significantly in January. A trend analysis shows this seasonality consistently over the past three years. Armed with this data, the store ramps up its holiday marketing and inventory planning while introducing a January clearance sale to mitigate the seasonal dip. This strategic adjustment boosts overall revenue and smooths cash flow throughout the year.

Scan code to download a sample trend analysis
https://finforfounders.com/trend-analysis

COST ANALYSIS

Cost Analysis focuses on understanding and optimizing the expenses that drive your business. By categorizing and scrutinizing costs, you can uncover inefficiencies, control expenses, and boost profitability. This analysis helps ensure that your resources are being used effectively to maximize returns.

Why It's Useful:

- Identifies opportunities for cost reduction without compromising quality
- Improves budgeting by providing a clear picture of where money is spent
- Highlights inefficiencies that can erode profit margins

Best Situations:

- Crucial when margins are tightening, and profitability is at risk
- Valuable for companies undergoing rapid growth to manage increasing operational costs
- Essential for periodic evaluations to ensure cost structures remain competitive

How to Perform Cost Analysis:

1. **Categorize Costs:** Break down expenses into fixed, variable, and indirect costs. Fixed costs are stable (e.g., office rent), variable costs fluctuate with service delivery (e.g., contractor fees), and indirect costs support operations (e.g., software subscriptions).

2. **Analyze Trends:** Compare costs over time to identify patterns, spikes, or decreases. For example, escalating advertising expenditures might signal the need to reevaluate the effectiveness of your campaigns.

3. **Benchmark:** Compare your cost structure with industry standards to uncover potential inefficiencies.

Cost Analysis example:

Consider a marketing agency where contractor expenses are rising due to frequent outsourcing of client projects. A cost analysis reveals that the agency's use of contractors for routine design work is driving up costs unnecessarily. By hiring an in-house designer for these tasks, the agency reduces variable costs and improves profit margins without sacrificing quality or turnaround times.

Scan code to download a sample cost analysis
https://finforfounders.com/cost-analysis

BREAK-EVEN ANALYSIS

Breakeven Analysis is a powerful tool to determine the point at which your revenue covers your costs. It provides clarity on the sales volume or revenue needed to avoid losses and helps founders make informed decisions about pricing, investments, and scaling.

Why It's Useful:

- Quantifies the sales volume required to achieve profitability
- Informs pricing and production decisions to ensure costs are covered
- Assesses the feasibility of new products or business lines

Best Situations:

- Critical for startups to understand when they will become profitable
- Useful when launching a new product or service to estimate required sales
- Valuable for established businesses to evaluate the impact of cost changes on profitability

How to Perform Breakeven Analysis:

1. **Identify Costs:** Separate fixed costs (e.g., rent, salaries) from variable costs (e.g., materials, shipping).
2. **Calculate the Contribution Margin:** Subtract variable costs per unit from the selling price per unit. This margin contributes to covering fixed costs and generating profit.
3. **Determine the Breakeven Point:** Divide total fixed costs by the contribution margin per unit to find the number of units needed to break even.

Break-Even Analysis example:

A SaaS company with $100,000 in fixed costs and a $50 contribution margin per subscription needs to sell 2,000 subscriptions to break even. By understanding this, they can set realistic sales targets and adjust marketing strategies accordingly.

Scan code to download a sample breakeven analysis
https://finforfounders.com/breakeven-analysis

ASSESSMENT: FINANCIAL ANALYSIS

Rate yourself on the following questions according to how satisfied you are with each. Insert a number between one and ten in each box and add them up. One means you are very dissatisfied; ten means you are very satisfied.

1. How satisfied are you with your ability to set realistic financial goals for your business? _____

2. How well does your financial planning process align with your long-term strategic goals? _____

3. How effective is your current method for creating annual financial plans and budgets? _____

4. How confident are you in your sales forecasting process? _____

5. How effectively do you track and analyze key performance indicators (KPIs) for your business? _____

6. How satisfied are you with your ability to forecast and manage cash flow? _____

7. How effectively do you use financial ratios to evaluate your business performance? _____

8. How satisfied are you with your ability to regularly update and adjust your financial plans based on business performance? _____

9. How confident are you in the quality of data used in your financial planning and analysis? _____

10. How well do you understand the financial metrics that impact your company's valuation? _____

Add up your score and write it here: _____

INTERPRETATION

Score range: 10 to 60
Needs Immediate Attention

You should prioritize investing time and resources into improving your financial planning and analysis function. Gaps in this area may hinder your company's growth and value.

Score range: 61 to 80
Making Progress

You have a foundational understanding of financial planning and analysis, but there's room for significant improvement to fully leverage it for business growth.

Score range: 81 to 100
Strong Performer

Your financial planning and analysis function is well-developed. Focus on fine-tuning your processes to maximize efficiency and long-term value.

Scan code to take the Planning & Analysis assessment online
https://finforfounders.com/planning-analysis

Pillar 4: Advice

7

"It's great to see you!" Lindsey stood up from the table to give Rachel a big hug as soon as she saw her friend approaching.

"Same here! I can't believe it's been months since we last met." Rachel took a step back to scan her friend from head to toe. "You look great. What's going on?"

Lindsey motioned for Rachel to sit, intentionally choosing the same table in the same restaurant they ate at the last time. "Things have gotten so much better at work—it's unbelievable! It's like a burden has been lifted from my shoulders since Mike and his team have taken over our finances."

"That's great news. I had a feeling you would enjoy working with him." Rachel paused to flag down the passing waiter. "Can we get a bottle of wine, please?" After the waiter nodded and noted her order, he left, and Rachel returned her focus to Lindsey. "I think this calls for a drink. My treat tonight."

"That's too kind of you," Lindsey smiled momentarily, caught up in the excitement of it all. But a look of concern slowly crept in.

"Something up?" asked Rachel.

"Yes." Lindsey reached across the table to put her hands over her friend's hand. "I'm just nervous about what comes next. Mike and Julien took me and Troy through so much stuff during our last meeting, and it all sounded great. But it was a lot to digest and in all of it he mentioned that it's time to bring in another team member."

"Mike is leaving you?"

"No, not at all! Mike had made it clear in the beginning he'd work to get us up and running, but at some point he'd need to hand off to another team member. I knew this was coming, but now that it's here I'm worried we'll lose momentum or even go backward.

"Mike said that with our growth, I need more time with a high-level financial executive that can work even more closely with me.

"I thought he wanted me to get a full-time Chief Financial Officer, which I don't think we need. He agreed that it would be overkill. But I would like more time with someone. So, I'm trying to balance the need for someone I can trust to continue this journey without the overhead of a full-time hire."

"What did he suggest?" said Rachel.

"He has somebody on his team that he can hand off to. A virtual CFO. He also said that at the right time if I felt I needed someone full-time he could help with that. If it does come to that, he could leave his team in place to support a full-time hire."

"Lindsey, that's a great problem to have."

"I know, and I also knew Mike had his business to run and he wasn't going to be available to me forever. But I am a nervous wreck. What if I get the wrong person? We finally got Troy in the right role and handling the tasks he is best suited for; I can't afford to get a bad CFO after all this hard work." Lindsey barely paused for a breath as Rachel looked on before continuing. "Would you be willing to come work for me?"

Rachel was flattered. Thankfully, the waiter had arrived with the bottle of wine and was in the process of pouring their glasses so she could formulate her next thoughts. "Lindsey, I would love to. But I'm not the right fit for you. I've been working at a big company my entire career and I really like it there…" Rachel put her hand out to stop Lindsey from interjecting as she was about to, "…you couldn't hire me full-time because I know you want to sell the business. If the new owners don't keep me on, I will never get my old job back. Plus, I'm a big-company person. I'm not sure I'd fit in."

Lindsey's face drooped at confirmation of what she already knew would be the case. It would not be fair to put her friend in that position for her own benefit. "Any suggestions?"

"Just ask Mike to make sure the person he has in mind is going to be a good fit for you. He won't leave you hanging—he's got a lot invested in this, too. There should be a long enough transition period where they are both working with you to make sure there is a clean handoff. If it's not working, let him know. He'll make sure you're happy with whoever fills that role."

"I'll do that." Lindsey said with relief.

* * *

Lindsey felt a familiar feeling of apprehension as she prepared to meet the new Virtual CFO. Mike worked quickly, lining up the meeting only a week after her dinner with Rachel.

Lindsey walked through the quiet common area as the time for her call approached. She had intentionally scheduled this call after business hours to avoid having anyone else listening in until she was sure the new CFO would be a good fit. With all the progress Troy had been making she was afraid of making him feel like he was getting replaced. So, she slipped inside her office, shut the door, and sat down at her computer. She still had a few minutes, so she reread Mike's last email to her:

> *"I am so glad you decided to take this step, Lindsey. Elliott has already helped many of our clients and I think he is going to be a great addition to your team. Julien has shared your most recent reports with him so that he can come to our first meeting fully prepared."*

Lindsey had blindly trusted Mike this entire time with no regrets, so she had no reason to second-guess this process. She clicked the meeting link. Mike and Elliott appeared. Mike started the meeting with an introduction to Elliott.

"'Hello!" Elliott had a cheery smile and an intuitive look in his eyes that was unmistakable even through a computer screen. "It's great to finally meet you, Lindsey."

"Same here," Lindsey replied. Her anxiety diminished. "Mike speaks very highly of you."

"Thank you," said Elliott.

Mike continued: "Elliott and I have worked together for many years. I thought he'd be a good fit because he just came off a project that was in a similar situation to yours. He guided them through an exit after being Virtual CFO for a couple years. The buyer installed their own team after the close, so Elliott's time freed up. We're lucky to have him because his experience is exactly what I think you need right now."

Lindsey liked what she heard. Elliott had exit experience, which aligned with her goals. He had longevity with his previous client. She could expect him to be around for a while. Although he hadn't spoken much yet, he seemed to be similar in demeanor to Mike.

"So how does this work exactly?" Lindsey was feeling better by the second.

"Not much different than it is now," Mike responded. "You and Elliott will set up a formal meeting cadence, whether it be weekly with the entire leadership team or one-on-one. He'll also be available for when you need some help with strategy or some analytical work to support decisions you need to make. I will attend the first few meetings to make sure the handoff is smooth. Then it will be up to you and Elliott. You and I will be checking in from time to time."

Mike went on, "Julien will continue generating all the reports from the data Troy is compiling every month, which will allow Elliott to do what a full-time CFO could do in far less time. Troy's help has been instrumental in our ability for us to do our work. He's excellent at what he does."

"Really?" Lindsey's said with surprise. She knew Troy was bought in on the new process, but didn't know he'd been excelling at it.

"Elliott has done a review of your situation. Before we let him go through it, there is something else we want to discuss with you today. Given all the progress we've seen thus far, and the noticeable impact on your profitability numbers, we think it would be wise to promote Troy to Controller and let him work directly under Elliott."

"Controller? Troy?" Lindsey loved the idea of recognizing Troy for all his contributions, but the title did give her pause. "Is he up for that? If he gets promoted, who is going to handle the data input?"

"That's the beauty of what we've created here, Lindsey." Mike spoke in a comforting tone. "Troy's old job has been so streamlined he's getting it done in a fraction of the time. We can get someone to handle transactional work, which frees Troy up to support you. With someone like Elliott mentoring him we have no doubt he would be make an even greater contribution."

"I'm on board with that," Lindsey admitted.

"Great," said Mike. "We'll walk you through roles and responsibilities as well as a recommended pay bump for him." Elliott took over the meeting and walked through some of his observations with Lindsey.

They wrapped up the call. Lindsey thought to herself that she went from zero corporate financial experts to three. Each had their own area of expertise. With this team in place, she was confident that whatever growth challenges lay ahead, they would be handled very well.

* * *

The greatest value a financial operation can bring to an organization is the ability to advise the founder on ways for the business to increase its value. This requires the other three pillars to be in place and functioning well. An advisor needs good data to support their recommendations.

Lindsey's company went from having an accounting department in disarray to one that is functioning smoothly and effectively. She is at the point where she wants more from her function than just the numbers. She wants to know how to interpret them so she can make better decisions. She wants her numbers to grow the value of her company, which ultimately leads to the greater freedom she seeks in her life. A strong CFO, either fractional or full-time, can give her this.

So how would Elliott make an impact? Several ways:

1. Bring clarity to growth plans
2. Establish structured mechanisms to provide advice
3. Introduce solid risk management systems
4. Ensure financial systems keep up with growth

First, he would bring clarity to her growth plans. Now that the business is growing in size and complexity, it is time to hire an expert who can help Lindsey navigate the company's economic future. Someone who can use data to support recommendations yet also apply their knowledge and experience to help her arrive at the best decision. It also has to be someone with the personality that meshes well with Lindsey.

The way Elliott advises her is through structured mechanisms like standing meetings, written reports, and analytics. He is also available to her for check-in meetings and other issues she may want to address. Many founders don't need a full-time CFO but are happy with having someone available, sometimes for just a few hours a month. With the team approach and well-defined roles, Lindsey knows when to go to Troy, Elliott, or Mike. She has plenty of support.

Risk management is a critical role for a CFO. Even the best made decisions can go wrong. Elliott will put in guardrails to identify when a decision is not working so the company can quickly develop an action plan and pivot to something that works. Think of a successful stock trader. The best ones put in stop losses so if an investment loses money, they cut their losses and move into a stock that can perform better. Companies that successfully scale have strong risk management systems in place.

Next, Elliott will ensure that her financial systems can keep up with growth. Growth adds complexity. His job will be to make sure that Lindsey continues to get accurate, timely data that is easy to understand.

Monthly Management Meeting

Monthly management meetings are a critical habit for founders who want to consistently achieve their objectives. These meetings serve as a structured checkpoint to ensure the company's financial and strategic goals remain on track. By setting aside dedicated time each month to review performance and plan ahead, founders can make informed decisions, address issues proactively, and maintain focus on long-term value creation. Without this discipline, it's easy for day-to-day operational demands to overshadow the bigger picture.

The agenda for these meetings is simple yet highly effective: review past performance and discuss what's coming next. To maintain consistency, set a fixed time each month—for example, the third Wednesday at 10 a.m.—and commit to it. Typically, these meetings last an hour, providing enough time to walk through the monthly financial report and discuss key issues. Quarterly meetings may extend to ninety minutes, as quarterly reviews often warrant deeper analysis of trends and performance metrics. These extended sessions are an excellent opportunity to perform comprehensive reviews and make any necessary larger adjustments to the company's plans.

A central component of the meeting is walking through the monthly financial report. The CFO or most senior financial leader runs the meeting, ensuring that discussions remain focused and actionable. Particular attention is given to negative variances: deviations from the plan that require immediate action. Think of the car dashboard: if your fuel gauge lights up, you know it's time to put more gas in the car.

Focusing on these discrepancies not only helps resolve current challenges but also provides valuable insights into potential root causes. Additionally, the meeting should elevate one or two strategic issues for further discussion. These could include topics like cash flow management, funding needs, or operational inefficiencies that have a significant impact on the business. Keep the Key Three objectives top of mind as you work through each meeting.

At the end of each meeting, it's important to prepare a list of the next steps to accomplish before the next session. This ensures accountability and keeps the team aligned with priorities. Adjustments to the plan are often discussed during these meetings, but they are usually minor tweaks based on recent performance. Major updates to the plan should generally be reserved for quarterly reviews when there is more data and context to support larger strategic shifts. This approach ensures the plan evolves thoughtfully and deliberately over time.

Over the months, these meetings become a powerful tool for founders to detect patterns in their business. By regularly reviewing performance and identifying trends, you will develop a deeper understanding of how operations drive the value of your company. These meetings instill habits that foster better decision-making, improve financial acumen, and build the discipline needed to scale successfully. For founders aiming to grow their business and increase its value, monthly management meetings are an indispensable practice.

Holding Your Team Accountable

Accountability is a crucial aspect in the success of any business, and it must be present at all levels across the entire organization. When it comes to your financial process, accountability begins by breaking monthly reports down by department and sharing them with department heads. These may be customized to each area to protect any confidential information. They report performance relevant to their department and ensure departmental performance aligns with overall corporate strategy.

Including key executives in the monthly management meeting is another critical step. This practice sets clear expectations for the financial performance they are responsible for delivering. When executives understand how their efforts contribute to the company's overall financial health, they are more likely to align their actions with broader business goals. Regular participation in these meetings keeps them informed of progress and highlights areas where they may need to course-correct. It's also an opportunity to discuss variances from the plan and collaboratively develop strategies to address them.

Tying incentive performance to the goals of the annual plan is an essential tool for driving accountability. Since the goals are financial in nature, the CFO can model the cash impact of incentive payments and ensure that meeting targets align with the ability of the company to fund them. This creates a powerful alignment between executive motivation and the company's financial success. When leaders see that their performance directly impacts both their rewards and the company's growth, it fosters a culture of accountability and results-driven decision-making. By managing these processes, the CFO helps the founder create a high-performing team that is focused on achieving the company's strategic objectives.

The Role of Your Chief Financial Officer

The best Chief Financial Officers make you smarter and more confident in your role as a founder. They act as a coach, someone who is easy to work with yet knows when to challenge you and when to step back. Temperament matters greatly in this relationship. You need someone who "gets" you, someone you feel comfortable with and trust implicitly. A great CFO is one of the few people in your organization—besides you—tasked with enhancing the value of your firm. This trust and alignment are essential to ensuring they can effectively support your vision and goals.

Beyond being a coach, a CFO is also an executive. They run the entire financial operation, managing the team that provides the data, reporting, and analytics you need to make the best decisions. Additionally, they act as a connector, linking you with other professionals who can support your business, such as sources of capital, legal experts, HR consultants, and insurance providers. This network further amplifies their value, ensuring your business has access to the right resources to scale and succeed.

Having a CFO gives a founder something they may have never had before: a reliable partner to help shoulder the burden of decision-making. While founders often rely on gut instinct and hustle to build their companies, a CFO brings a disciplined approach to evaluating options. They provide clarity in moments of uncertainty and help forecast the financial implications of different scenarios, whether it's launching a new product, securing funding, or acquiring another business. This guidance ensures the founder is always prepared to make decisions based on data rather than guesswork.

Moreover, the CFO's advice extends beyond just numbers. They offer perspective on how financial decisions ripple across the organization. For example, a cost-cutting measure might improve short-term profitability but could impact morale or long-term growth potential. A seasoned CFO helps founders think through these tradeoffs and make choices that align with the company's broader strategy and values. Their ability to combine analytical rigor with strategic insight is invaluable for founders navigating complex decisions.

Over time, the partnership with a CFO makes a founder more forward thinking and less reactive. Founders often find themselves consumed by the day-to-day demands of running a business. A CFO helps lift their perspective to focus on long-term goals and patterns that drive value. They bring discipline to planning and execution, ensuring that the founder's vision is backed by a solid financial foundation. This shift allows the founder to operate with greater confidence and clarity, knowing that their decisions are informed by expert guidance and are more likely to result in positive financial performance.

Finally, a CFO provides peace of mind. Knowing a trusted advisor is managing the financial side of the business allows the founder to focus on other critical areas, such as developing talent and new business. With a CFO by their side, founders can lead with confidence, knowing they have a partner dedicated to enhancing the value of their firm and helping them achieve their vision.

When to Hire a CFO

In Lindsey's story, she had the benefit of working with Mike and getting his insight and advice as it pertained to the reorganization of the accounting department and the need for a CFO. How did she get to the point where she needed a CFO? There are typically five signs:

1. Growing rapidly
2. Spending too much time "in" the business and not "on" the business
3. Lacking a roadmap for growth
4. Raising capital or exiting the business
5. Missing proper cost controls

When a company is growing rapidly, the financial operations can quickly become overwhelming. Perhaps transactions aren't getting entered in a timely fashion, invoicing is going out later than usual, or financial statements are taking longer to prepare. A CFO can step in to stabilize a shaky accounting operation, implementing new processes and controls while cleaning up historical data. With these foundational improvements, a CFO enables the company to generate accurate data, which is critical for analytics, sound strategic development, and crisp execution.

For many business owners, rapid growth also means they are spending too much time working "in" the business instead of "on" it. Founders often find themselves bogged down with tedious bookkeeping and operational finance tasks, leaving little room for strategic decision-making or growth initiatives. A CFO takes on the responsibility of managing the company's finances, sharing the burden, and freeing up the founder to focus on driving innovation, building relationships, and scaling the business.

A growing business also needs a clear roadmap for future growth, and this requires robust financial planning and analytics. Developing these tools goes beyond the capabilities of basic accounting teams. A CFO has the expertise to create sophisticated models, forecasts, and strategies that help the business prioritize opportunities and allocate resources effectively. By providing insights into where the business is headed and what it needs to get there, a CFO ensures the company stays on track toward its long-term goals.

When it comes to raising capital or preparing for an exit, a CFO becomes indispensable. They know how to engage with investors and lenders, understanding what these stakeholders need and positioning the company to exceed their expectations. Whether it's preparing financial statements, building a compelling pitch, or addressing due diligence questions, a CFO brings the expertise and credibility that give external partners confidence in the founder's business's financial operation and its leadership.

Cost control is another area where a CFO adds significant value. As companies grow, expenses can spiral out of control without proper oversight. A CFO systematically analyzes expenses, identifies areas of waste or inefficiency, and develops cost-saving strategies. By implementing these measures, they not only improve EBITDA but also ensure that the company is operating as efficiently as possible, maximizing the return on every dollar spent.

ASSESSMENT: ADVICE

Rate yourself on the following questions according to how satisfied you are with each. Insert a number between one and ten in each box and add them up. If you do not have a CFO then use the most senior financial person on your team as a substitute. One means you are very dissatisfied; ten means you are very satisfied.

1. Do you feel the advice you receive from your CFO clearly aligns with your business growth plans and objectives? _____

2. Are there structured mechanisms in place, such as standing meetings or detailed reports, to ensure you consistently receive actionable advice? _____

3. Is your CFO available when you need them, and do they make it easy for you to address ad-hoc concerns? _____

4. Are you satisfied with the systems in place to identify and mitigate financial risks in your business? _____

5. Do you feel your CFO understands you and communicates advice in a manner that matches your personal and professional style? _____

6. Do you trust your CFO to provide clarity during moments of uncertainty and to help you weigh the financial implications of various decisions? _____

7. Does your advisor help you consider the broader impacts of financial decisions on your company's long-term strategy and values? _____

8. Has working with your advisor helped you become more forward-thinking and less reactive in your approach to business decisions? _____

9. Do you feel more confident in your role as a founder because of the advice you receive from your CFO? _____

10. Does having a CFO give you peace of mind, knowing the financial side of your business is managed effectively, allowing you to focus on other areas? _____

Add up your score and write it here: _____

INTERPRETATION

Score Range: 10 to 60
Reassess Your Advisory Relationship

Your satisfaction with the advice you receive is low. It may be time to reconsider whether the current advisor or structure is the right fit for your needs.

Score Range: 61 to 80
Room for Improvement

Your satisfaction with the advice you receive is moderate. While there are positive aspects, there may be opportunities for improvement in the clarity, delivery, or relevance of the advice.

Score Range: 81 to 100
High Satisfaction

You are highly satisfied with the advice you are receiving. Your advisor appears to be adding significant value and aligning with your business needs effectively.

Scan code to take the Advice assessment online
https://finforfounders.com/advice

8

Managing Taxes

"*I hate this time of year!*" Lindsey thought to herself while gathering all her tax documents. Troy had offered to help but Lindsey knew it would be best for her to spend the time, as unpleasant as it was, getting a few minutes alone with Abe. He had been doing their taxes from day one and Lindsey felt like she saw less and less of him as the years went on. In the beginning, she watched every dollar. She wanted to know about every single tax deduction.

For the last few years, Lindsey skipped her bi-annual meetings with Abe entirely. She got tied up in other things with the business and didn't see any issues with her taxes. It was a cost of doing business and she had other things to do.

This year, after having worked with Mike and his team, things were going to be different. One of the first things Elliott had warned her about increased income was that their tax situation would likely change. He wanted to share some strategies he had seen work with other clients, but he confessed he was not a tax professional. He advised Lindsey to go see Abe first and get a handle on what her liability looked like.

"Come in," came the reply from the other side of the door shortly after Lindsey knocked.

She pushed the door open, leading with her shoulder to keep the door from swinging back against the weight of the piles of folders and boxes cluttering the floor of the office. "You're going to wind up buried in here if you're not careful," Lindsey joked with Abe. She maneuvered her way through the obstacle course of paperwork so that she could place some documents on Abe's desk.

Abe peered up from the ledger he was scribbling in, narrow eyes barely visible over the rims of his thick glasses. "Live by the numbers, die by the numbers." He chuckled at his dry accountant's humor. "Have a seat."

Lindsey accepted the invitation to sit at the only chair not piled high with manilla folders. "Glad to see some things never change." She noticed how much paper was in Abe's office.

Abe sat back, face growing more serious. "But some things do. Based on the summary of your financials Troy emailed me, it looks like you had a banner year."

"That's a good thing isn't it?" Lindsey asked hesitantly, sensing what was coming next.

"The IRS is sure going to think so. You know I've always done my best in the past to help you reduce that exposure as much as possible. We usually spend down your cash at the end of the year to reduce your cash taxes. I'm not sure if it will be enough this time. You're still going to owe a lot of money.

"And I guess that's a good thing," Abe said in a backhanded way as he flipped through a stack of papers on his desk. "Because you are going to need a considerable chunk of the cash to pay estimated taxes in a couple weeks."

"How much is considerable?" Lindsey emphasized the last word and leaned forward.

"More than half the cash on the balance sheet you just sent me."

Lindsey would have fallen off her chair if not for the state of shock she was in. "How could that happen? There ought to be something I can do."

"It happened," Abe said, "because you didn't inform me during the year that you were doing so well. You didn't pay enough estimated taxes this year. Not only do you have a big tax bill, but you may be subject to penalties and interest because you didn't pay enough estimated taxes. You should have kept those meetings with me."

Lindsey was taken aback by Abe's harshness. He had always been pleasant. Now he was edgy—and looked exhausted. Other than those meetings, she never heard from Abe. Maybe if he reached out a little more she would have found this out sooner and could have done something about it. Abe looked from Lindsey to his watch then back again to Lindsey. "Well, there's twenty days left in the fiscal year. You can always find something to spend the money on. This way you are investing in the company and not the government."

Lindsey walked to her car in disbelief. In the short time since Elliott had joined the team she had never had the need to use his personal number he gave her for emergencies. This seemed to fit the bill as much as any situation she could think of. "If this isn't a good time, I can wait until our meeting Friday," she said, as Elliott promptly answered.

"Sounds like you might not make it that long." Elliott's voice was reassuring on the other end of the line. "I take it that things didn't go well with the accountant?"

"I owe over two hundred thousand dollars, Elliott. How the heck does that happen?"

"Yes, that's a terrible surprise, but there is some good news here," Elliot replied. "The good news is that we found this out with some time left in the year and a little over a month before the payment is due. There may be some things we can do to reduce your taxes."

"Like what? Giving it away?" She realized mid-sentence she was coming across as harshly to Elliott as Abe had just been with her.

"There are plenty of strategies we have seen work with other clients. Retirement plan contributions, health savings accounts…"

"Investing the money back into the business?" Abe's words replayed in her head as she blurted out the statement.

There was a noticeable pause at the other end of the line before Elliott continued. "Yes, the right investments will reduce your taxable income. But Lindsey," he paused again for gravity, "there is time left in the year. Why don't we go through all the options on Friday and make the best decision?"

Just as Lindsey was set to ask Elliott if they could push the meeting up a day or two, the caller ID on her phone flashed with the name of her biggest client. In her time with Abe, she had been ignoring her phone. She had called Elliott right away. Now she noticed she had missed several text messages from the client. This call was not a good sign. "I'm sorry, Elliott, a client is calling, and I need to take it. Let's regroup Friday for sure."

* * *

This is not a chapter about how to pay less in taxes. There are plenty of books about that. This is a chapter on the influence taxes have on founders and how those influences could lead to decisions that might hurt your company's growth. Balancing tax reduction with investing in the business are tradeoffs founders make all the time. We want to introduce some common situations so you can be better informed should you be facing the same circumstances.

Problems arise when business owners focus too aggressively on tax reduction or are not paying enough attention to the tax implications of a company with growing profits. Lindsey had fallen into a pattern of passing off her tax responsibilities to Troy and Abe. When growth was lower and there was less at stake, Lindsey was comfortable delegating this task, paying what she was told to pay and following their lead.

> **FINSIGHT**
>
> **Don't spend down your cash at the end of the year just to reduce your tax liability. You may need that cash next year and you could be setting yourself up for an even bigger tax liability in the future.**

Here is a common example: many business owners are advised to spend down their cash at the end of the year to reduce their tax liability. This is terrible advice.

First, the tax burden is not reduced, it's merely pushed into the next year. If your profits continue growing, you'll have to repeat the same exercise with even more cash every year until such a point as it is no longer sustainable—and that day will come.

Next, that cash you spend at the end of the year may be needed to fund operations or new initiatives in the new year. We've seen founders tap into their lines of credit and incur interest expenses because they prematurely spent too much of their cash.

Finally, if you are looking for a loan, your bank is going to want to see year-end balance sheets from the past couple of years. If they consistently see a very low cash balance they will assume you are at higher risk of default. Cash matters a great deal to them. That loan you apply for may cost more money, if it is written for you at all.

One of the shocks to most business owners who suddenly experience high-profit growth is how much taxation really starts to matter. To compound that problem, they are likely also suffering from some other bad habits:

- Waiting too long to get their tax preparer their documentation
- Not keeping their tax preparer updated on financial performance throughout the year
- Working with a tax preparer who does not specialize in business returns for *growth stage business owners*

There are strategies to help founders, but they require the expertise of tax professionals skilled in situations like yours. Let's look at four different areas that can help guide you toward making better tax decisions.

Impact of Company Type on Taxation

Many founders do not give much thought to the different options for legal entity status when founding their companies. Those that start as a side business are often just sole proprietors. The business owner operates under their own name and has no separation of taxation or liability from the company. There is nothing wrong with this—until the company starts to grow.

How your company is organized determines not only how you pay taxes, but also when and how much. Different organization options also provide for different legal protections, so at some point it will be important to consult a tax professional and lawyer to determine what the best option is for your company. It is also worth noting here that you do not have to be locked into the entity type forever. As different factors in your business evolve it is important to make sure your legal structure is still the most beneficial. Below are the three most common company types.

LIMITED LIABILITY COMPANY (LLC)

The LLC is often the first stop for many founders due to its simplicity and the protection it provides. There are some strings attached.

From a tax perspective, it's straightforward: profits "pass through" to you, the owner, and show up on your personal tax return via a K-1 form. But there's a catch: as the owner, you're on the hook for self-employment taxes, covering both the employee and employer portions of Social Security and Medicare. This means your tax burden could be higher than you expect, especially as profits grow. While this structure makes sense when you're just starting, it's worth asking whether it still serves you as your company scales.

S-CORPORATION

Many LLC owners elect to be taxed as an S-Corporation to reduce their self-employment tax burden. Here's how it works: only the salaries you pay yourself as a W-2 employee are subject to self-employment taxes. The remaining profits avoid that extra tax layer and flow to you through a K-1.

But there's a trade-off—more paperwork and stricter rules. You'll need to set a "reasonable salary" for yourself, and that can sometimes feel like navigating a gray area with the IRS. There are restrictions on stock ownership. Still, for many founders, the S-Corp provides a tax-efficient middle ground as their business moves from startup to growth stage.

C-CORPORATION

For founders aiming to scale their company significantly, a C-Corporation might become inevitable. This is the "Big Leagues" and is how all publicly traded companies are structured. It also comes with big tax bills.

Unlike LLCs and S-Corps, a C-Corp is its own tax-paying entity. This means double taxation: the company pays taxes on its net income, and shareholders (including you) pay taxes again on dividends.

While this sounds like a founder's worst nightmare, it comes with its own set of advantages—access to institutional investors, the ability to offer stock options to employees, and a smoother path to selling to a buyer or going public. Still, the double-taxation burden is not one to take lightly, especially if you're in growth mode and need every dollar to fuel expansion.

WORK WITH ADVISORS WHO GET YOUR GROWTH STAGE

Surround yourself with advisors who specialize in companies like yours. Tax law is complicated, but it can also be leveraged to your advantage if you work with the right people. Whether it's determining the best salary to pay yourself in an S-Corp or figuring out when to make the leap to a C-Corp, expert guidance can save you headaches and money. And most importantly, it can help you focus on scaling your business without losing sleep over tax decisions.

Paying Taxes on a Cash Basis

In Chapter 4, we covered why you need to keep your books on an accrual basis. Many founders get confused by this when it comes to taxes. They ask how they can keep their books on an accrual basis yet pay taxes on a cash basis. This section clears up that confusion.

When forming a company, founders frequently rely on their tax preparers to set up their accounting systems. Tax preparers tend to favor cash basis accounting for its simplicity and alignment with the tax payment process. Under cash basis accounting, taxes are calculated based only on the cash received during the fiscal year. This approach ensures businesses only pay taxes on cash they earned, so they can pay taxes with cash on hand. It avoids situations in accrual accounting, where unpaid sales invoices count against revenue. Those invoices generated no cash to pay taxes on the income they generated.

For example, imagine invoicing a large customer for $50,000 in December but not receiving payment until January. If your books are on an accrual basis and your taxes are calculated the same way, you would owe taxes on that $50,000 for the fiscal year that just ended, even though you haven't received the cash. Cash basis accounting avoids this scenario by only taxing income when it is physically collected. This works well for smaller businesses or those just starting out, but as explained in Chapter 4, it becomes limiting as companies grow.

Fortunately, businesses don't have to choose one method exclusively. You can maintain accrual basis books for managing your business while still calculating taxes on a cash basis. Note that you are *not* keeping two sets of books. You are changing the *basis* by which you are reporting your financials.

FINSIGHT

You can maintain accrual basis in your accounting software and prepare tax returns on a cash basis. There is a section on your tax return that reconciles the two.

As we touched on in Chapter 4, you can reconcile the tax return basis to your internal financial reporting through a section of the tax return known as Schedule M-1. It's vital to ensure your accountant completes this reconciliation accurately, as it connects your books to your tax return without requiring two sets of books. This allows growing companies to maintain financial clarity while managing their tax burdens effectively.

Taxes and Operating Decisions

Taxes are an inevitable cost of doing business, but they should not dictate how you run your company. While it's important to consider the tax implications of certain decisions, too many founders allow tax avoidance to overly influence certain decisions. This can lead to short-sighted strategies that hurt long-term growth and profitability. Taxes are just one piece of the puzzle and allowing them to overly influence your decision-making can cause more harm than good. Instead, prioritize the needs of your business and its financial health above all else.

Many tax avoidance strategies are deferring, rather than reducing, taxes. While deferrals can provide short-term cash flow relief, they often come with strings attached. Decisions made to defer taxes now may lead to unwelcome surprises later when the bill comes due. For example, if you've been deferring taxes aggressively, selling your business could become more complicated. Unresolved tax liabilities might scare off potential buyers or lead to a larger tax bill at closing, potentially diminishing the value of your hard-earned exit.

Ultimately, your operating decisions should align with the broader goals of your business, not just your tax strategy. Taxes are a factor—an important one—but not the only one. By maintaining a balanced approach and understanding the long-term implications of your tax-related decisions, you can ensure that your business remains financially healthy and positioned for growth, no matter what the tax authorities have in store.

Avoiding Surprises

Avoiding unpleasant surprises from your tax preparer begins with preparation, communication, and a proactive approach to your financial responsibilities. Too often, founders find themselves blindsided during tax season because they failed to anticipate potential issues or fully engage with their tax preparer throughout the year. Consider these real-world examples:

- A founder did not provide prior year financial data to their tax preparer until shortly before the tax filing deadline. They were hit with a big tax bill and had no chance to correct it because the tax year was long over.

- A founder wanted to make a year-end contribution to a retirement plan based on their W2 salary. In the prior year, they reduced their salary and took higher distributions. Their ability to contribute to their retirement plan was greatly reduced.

- A founder took out distributions from their company that exceeded the company's net income. They took out a big loan earlier in the year to fund the distribution. The founder had a "basis problem" and had to pay additional taxes.

By taking the following steps, you can minimize these surprises and maintain better control over your company's financial health.

1. Maintain Accurate and Up-to-Date Records

Good bookkeeping is the foundation of avoiding tax headaches. Maintain your books in accordance with the practices we outlined in Chapter 5. The more organized your records are, the fewer chances there are for unexpected tax liabilities to arise.

2. Stay on Top of Estimated Tax Payments

Founders often underestimate the importance of quarterly tax payments, leading to unexpected penalties and interest. Work with your tax preparer to calculate accurate estimates based on your current financial performance.

Ask your accountant how "Safe Harbor" may benefit you when determining estimated payments. Safe harbor sets a minimum level of estimated payments based upon the prior year's liability. Making them shields you from penalties and interest if your actual tax liability exceeded your estimates.

Most importantly, make your estimated tax payments on time to avoid unpleasant surprises when your annual tax return is filed.

3. Understand Your Tax Reduction Strategies

Founders want to pay their fair share of taxes and will take advantage of any programs that may be offered for businesses like theirs. From R&D tax credits to contributions to retirement accounts, there is no shortage of opportunities to reduce your company's tax burden. What is important to understand is that these tax reduction programs come with strings attached. There are often exclusions and other stipulations that may reduce your benefit because of your unique situation.

For example, if you want to aggressively contribute to your retirement, it comes at the cost of providing retirement benefits to your staff and getting them to participate at certain levels. These contributions will lower your overall profitability and thus your taxes, but it will cost you cash. You may want something that allows you the flexibility to contribute less during lower profit years, so you are not locked into spending money you do not have.

Take the time to sit with your advisor to work through these details. Have them provide you in writing how a certain strategy is designed to work and what specific aspects of your situation entitle you to a benefit—as well as any changes that could disqualify you from that benefit.

4. Build a Strong Relationship with Your Tax Preparer

Founders sometimes put off tax consultations until it's too late, leading to rushed decisions and missed opportunities. Here are common problems caused by delays getting information to your tax preparer:

- **Unclaimed Deductions or Credits:** Waiting until the last minute may cause you to overlook tax-saving opportunities that require documentation or pre-planning.
- **Cash Flow Crunches:** Delayed consultations can lead to surprise liabilities you didn't budget for, potentially straining your finances.
- **Errors in Financial Reporting:** Rushing through your tax filings increases the risk of mistakes, which can lead to audits or penalties.
- **Missed Deadlines:** Procrastination might mean you miss filing deadlines, incurring additional penalties.

A good working relationship with your tax preparer can make all the difference. Choose someone who understands your industry, your business model, and who works with founders. Communicate openly, ask questions, and provide them with all necessary information in a timely manner.

Keep in mind that you have one tax preparer, and they may have hundreds of clients. They are more engaged with people they enjoy working with. Be one of those people by:

1. Scheduling meetings with them when they aren't busy. Their schedules get less busy a couple weeks after the big tax deadlines of March, April, September and October each year.
2. Prepare for those meetings by sending any information they request at least a week in advance.
3. Communicate clearly your current situation and what you need from them.
4. Pay them on time or earlier. If fees seem excessive, ask what you can do to bring them down.

5. Review Tax Returns Thoroughly

Before signing off on your tax return, review it carefully with your preparer. A business tax return is dense. Read through it and take notes to ask your preparer. Remember, even if a professional prepared your return, you are ultimately responsible for its accuracy.

ASSESSMENT: TAXES

Rate yourself on the following questions according to how satisfied you are with each. Insert a number between one and ten in each box and add them up. One means you are very dissatisfied; ten means you are very satisfied.

1. How satisfied are you with your understanding of how taxes influence key financial decisions in your business? _____

2. How confident are you in your ability to balance tax reduction strategies with investing in business growth? _____

3. How effectively do you communicate financial performance updates to your tax preparer throughout the year? _____

4. How well does your current tax advisor specialize in business returns for growth-stage companies? _____

5. How satisfied are you with your company's legal structure in terms of its tax efficiency and alignment with growth goals? _____

6. How effectively does your current financial system reconcile tax reporting with internal financial reporting? _____

7. How proactive are you in addressing potential tax liabilities or opportunities before the end of the fiscal year? _____

8. How satisfied are you with your company's ability to maintain accurate and up-to-date financial records for tax purposes? _____

9. How well do your operating decisions prioritize long-term growth over short-term tax deferrals? _____

10. How strong is your working relationship with your tax preparer in terms of collaboration, communication, and trust? _____

Add up your score and write it here: _____

INTERPRETATION

Score range: 10 to 60
Low Engagement

You may need to significantly invest time and resources into understanding and improving your financial planning and tax strategies. Immediate action is required to avoid negative impacts on business growth.

Score Range: 61 to 80
Moderate Engagement

You have some understanding and processes in place but need to strengthen financial and tax functions to better align with growth-stage business needs.

Score Range: 81 to 100
High Engagement

You demonstrate strong management of financial planning and tax strategies. You are well-positioned for continued growth but should maintain vigilance for further optimization opportunities.

Scan code to take the Taxes assessment online
https://finforfounders.com/taxes

Implementation

9

"Have you seen Lindsey?" Yvette softly asked Troy through his partially ajar office door.

"She should be in her office, no?" Troy asked in confusion since Lindsey had been uncharacteristically quiet and secluded in her office the last few weeks.

"I'm not sure. She's been short with me lately and spending a lot of time in her office with the door closed. Now she's not replying to my emails or instant messages." Yvette waited for Troy to give her his full attention. "The lights are out in her office and the blinds are drawn."

"Can you please let her know Mike and Elliott have both been trying to get a hold of her?"

That sealed it for Troy. He stood up and announced, "I'll go check on her." Troy stood with a spring in his step.

"Julien was looking for her the other day as well and she told me she would get right back to her." Troy slipped by on his way down the hall toward Lindsey's office, waving her off to signify he would handle it.

"Go away," Lindsey shouted from the other side of her closed door in response to Troy's soft tapping.

"Not going to happen, Lindsey. I know when something's wrong so you can either let me in to talk about it or we can do it through the door for everyone else to hear."

It only took a moment for the sounds of footsteps to echo on the other side of the door before the lock clicked open and Lindsey ushered him inside. "I swear everything is okay," she offered, futilely.

"Then why are Mike and Elliott having difficulty getting in touch with you?" Troy asked. He had a fairly good idea something was up based upon some financial information Julien recently shared with him.

Lindsey plopped into her chair, exhaling in exasperation. "I made an executive decision I don't think they are going to like."

"Like…" Troy tried leading Lindsey and her face confirmed what he was about to ask, "…or know about?" When she didn't answer, he pressed the issue. "Look, it's your company so of course I'll support whatever it is you want to do. But since you've brought Mike and his team in, things have dramatically improved around here. You seem to have been okay with what we are doing. So, I'm very curious about what you are up to and what you are so afraid of?"

Lindsey motioned for him to sit, then leaned in close as if the walls were listening. "Remember the complaints we were getting from some of our customers about inefficiencies in our applicant screening process and the money they were losing because of onboarding and turnover?" As Troy nodded, Lindsey continued. "They were threatening to leave if we couldn't figure out how to streamline the process."

"But they haven't left." Troy struggled to connect the dots.

"Remember that app we were going to build a few months back and ruled out because of the cost?"

Concern washed over Troy's face. "You mean the one that was going to cost at least several hundred thousand dollars to build out and we still weren't sure it was going to work? That one?"

Lindsey stared at him blankly in response.

"What did Elliott say when you mentioned it to him?" Troy implored.

Lindsey continued her blank stare.

"Mike?" Desperation was increasingly evident in his voice.

Lindsey remained quiet.

"Julien?"

"I met with Abe and learned I was going to have a high tax liability due to the extra profits we were making this year. The owner of the application development firm called and said if we signed up before year end and made some advance payments he'd give us a discount. I figured we were going to do it anyway, so I just got it started earlier."

Troy was stunned. Lindsey deliberately did what only she, as founder, could do. She circumvented all the controls, processes, and technology they put in place to prevent this exact thing from happening.

As founder, she had the authority to do that. It's her business. But in doing this she sent a clear signal that those structures applied to others and not to her. The message she'd send to the team when word got out would be terrible. Troy feared Mike would resign and pull his team when he heard this. He put his fears aside and dealt with the matter at hand. "Okay, where are you on this?"

"Well, I've already paid them about $300,000."

If Troy was stunned before, now he would go completely into shock. "What? How? I didn't see those payments get made!" he nearly shouted.

"I paid them with personal funds and was going to have the company reimburse me when I told you about it."

Troy waited a full thirty seconds before responding. She knew what she was doing was wrong and she hid it from him. In all their years working together, she had never done anything like this. "What else do I need to know?" Troy demanded.

"We're behind schedule. And they are asking for another three hundred grand. I was holed up in here trying to figure out what to do when you barged in."

"I'm going to set up a meeting with Mike and Elliott." It came out as a command, but Troy still lingered in the office long enough for Lindsey to nod her acquiescence before heading out to make the call.

* * *

Lindsey knew what she did was wrong. She deliberately violated the controls and processes that were put in place to prevent exactly what she did from happening. As a founder, only she has that authority. She thought she could paper over it later; however, she sent a clear signal that certain rules did not apply to her. This could have a devastating impact on her business. Nobody wants to work for somebody who won't obey their own rules.

Founders can commit to doing the hard work of scaling their companies. If they are unwilling to change themselves, however, they can quickly undo that work. While that is a risk in any founder-led company, it doesn't mean that the company should not implement the changes necessary to ensure the continued growth everyone wants to achieve.

Building a top-tier financial operation for your business isn't just about adding one tool, process, or person. It's about creating a balanced ecosystem where sound processes, technology, and competent people work in harmony.

Processes ensure the integrity of your financial data and establish proper controls. Technology streamlines these processes, eliminating inefficiencies and improving accuracy. And none of it works without the right professionals with the expertise and discipline to execute the work. Success in implementing a financial operation requires all three elements working together seamlessly. Most importantly, it requires the founder to demonstrate their commitment by living within the new systems established by the company.

> **FINSIGHT**
>
> A committed founder, competent people, proven processes, and effective technology are required to deliver a top-tier financial operation.

Creating this requires an investment of both time and money. Too many founders see finance as a cost center and not the key driver of the company's valuation that it is. What other department keeps score on how your business is performing financially? Who else can guide founders on investments to make and provide feedback on how well those investments pay off?

Many founders think salespeople are the most valued employees because without sales there is no business. If those sales are not profitable, however, then there is no business. With finance's focus on profitability and cash, only that team can provide you with the clarity you need to ensure you have a *sustainable* business.

How much you'll need to invest depends on where your financial operation stands today and what your long-term goals are. Do you need to fix glaring issues, or are you building toward a future vision? The good news is that you can start seeing tangible results in as little as thirty days when you focus on the right areas.

Process and Control Are Necessities

In growth-stage companies, robust financial processes and controls are not just a luxury—they're a necessity. As businesses grow to, say, $10 million annual revenue, the complexities of financial management are very different than when the company was making $1 million in sales. Unfortunately, many founders like Lindsey find themselves caught in the weeds of processes that should have evolved long ago. This not only hampers operational efficiency but also impacts cash flow and scalability.

Financial professionals emphasize processes and controls because they create a framework of checks and balances. These systems ensure data is accurate, compliant with Generally Accepted Accounting Principles (GAAP, a US-based set of accounting rules), and transparent. They also introduce redundancy, allowing for multiple verification methods to catch errors and prevent dishonesty. Without these safeguards, even routine tasks like invoicing can become major bottlenecks.

Take Lindsey's business, for example. Initially, Lindsey handled invoicing herself, finding it a great way to keep tabs on the business. But as the company grew, her hands-on approach became a liability. The invoicing process was cumbersome, with Lindsey reviewing milestones, consulting project managers, and making ad hoc adjustments. Invoices were created in Excel then transferred to their accounting system. This approach delayed billing and stretched cash flow timelines, sometimes pushing payment collection well beyond the thirty days they hoped to collect.

Mike and his team introduced a billing schedule prepared at the start of each project. He shifted responsibility to the project manager, who was closer to the work. He showed Troy how to use the accounting system to create invoices that were both customer-ready and internally documented. The new process eliminated Excel templates and ensured invoices were reviewed and sent promptly, with disputed items flagged for the next cycle. Lindsey's role was reduced to reviewing monthly reports, freeing her to focus on growing the business.

> **FINSIGHT**
>
> **Segregation of duties, the division of financial responsibilities, improves accuracy and reduces fraud.**

The results were transformative. Invoices went out faster, cash flow improved, and the workload was divided among the team, reducing bottlenecks. This segregation of duties—a cornerstone of accounting controls—ensured no single person could initiate, approve, and review the same transaction, improving accuracy and reducing fraud. By leveraging the accounting system's capabilities, the team moved from manual spreadsheets to an integrated solution, making data accessible and actionable.

Invoicing is just one example. The same approach can be applied to all financial functions, from accounts payable to payroll. Proper processes and controls aren't just about compliance—they're also about setting the foundation for scalable, sustainable growth.

Technology Stack

For years, founders of growth-stage companies believed that investing in an Enterprise Resource Planning (ERP) system was the natural step to scale effectively. ERPs promised a one-stop shop for managing everything from inventory to customer relationships to financials.

Reality was often less rosy. These systems were expensive to implement and maintain, with upfront costs that could swallow a sizable portion of a small business's budget and ongoing annual maintenance fees of at least twenty percent of the initial license cost. They also tended to be overly complex, offering functionality far beyond what most founders needed, especially in the early growth stage. To make matters worse, many ERPs require dedicated installations and clunky access methods, leaving founders frustrated rather than empowered.

The growth in cloud-based apps over the past decade offers a far more practical alternative for founders: the "best of breed" approach. Instead of committing to a single monolithic ERP system, founders can now assemble a suite of specialized, browser-based apps tailored to their needs.

These apps are not only more affordable, thanks to subscription-based pricing models, but also more flexible and user-friendly. By integrating these tools with a cloud-based general ledger like QuickBooks Online, founders can create a powerful, scalable system without the bloat of an ERP. Whether it's timekeeping, financial planning, analytics, or CRM, these apps are designed to communicate seamlessly with the general ledger, moving companies away from clunky spreadsheets and into streamlined, integrated operations.

Now, the question becomes: how can founders deploy this technology? There are three paths to consider:

Do It Yourself

Founders with a DIY mindset might attempt to build and integrate their tech stack on their own. While this approach seems cost-effective upfront, it often leads to hidden challenges.

Selecting the right apps, ensuring seamless integration, and troubleshooting issues require expertise and time—resources that are usually stretched thin in a growth-stage company. Without a clear plan and technical know-how, a founder risks creating a patchwork system that's inefficient, difficult to scale, and prone to errors. Moreover, keeping everything updated and secure falls squarely on the owner's shoulders.

Hire a Consultant

Bringing in a consultant to implement and train your team on a custom-built system is a middle-ground approach. The benefit here is clear: you get expert guidance to design and deploy a stack tailored to your business needs.

Consultants also ensure your team is trained to use the tools effectively. However, this doesn't mean you're off the hook. You'll still be responsible for maintaining the system, handling updates, and ensuring new team members receive the necessary training. Over time, these ongoing tasks can become a significant burden, especially as your company grows and evolves.

Outsource

The final option is to partner with an outsourced firm like Lindsey did and leverage their pre-built tech stack. This approach eliminates the need for the company to build and maintain its own system. The outsourced firm handled all aspects of the technology stack, allowing Lindsey to focus on growing her business rather than managing tech infrastructure.

The downside? The founder has to find a provider whose system matches their needs. Then the company is tied to that system. If the relationship ends, the founder needs a plan to ensure continuity, as transitioning to a new system can be disruptive.

Each path has its trade-offs. DIY offers control but demands technical expertise, hiring a consultant balances customization with ongoing responsibility, and outsourcing simplifies operations but requires careful provider selection. The key is to align your choice with your company's resources, expertise, and growth trajectory.

HOW AI FITS INTO THE TECHNOLOGY STACK

AI is revolutionizing the way businesses manage their financial operations, offering capabilities that go far beyond traditional software. Its role in automation and prediction is particularly compelling for growth-stage companies looking to scale efficiently and make better decisions.

Automation

AI excels at handling repetitive, time-consuming tasks with precision. Take financial reconciliations as an example. In the past, your finance team might spend thirty minutes a day manually matching credit card transactions with bank deposits, categorizing revenues and fees, and preparing journal entries. With AI, this process is reduced to seconds. AI tools can fetch data, update datasets, generate journal entries, and even upload detailed records to your document management system—all with minimal human intervention. *The result?* A process that's faster, more accurate, and scalable, freeing up many hours a month for your team to focus on more value-added activities.

Prediction

AI's predictive algorithms empower founders to plan with greater confidence. AI can analyze historical performance, benchmark data from similar companies, and incorporate strategic objectives to generate sophisticated financial models. You can prompt it to provide its source data and explain why it feels its prediction is the best one for you.

These models, complete with assumptions and constraints, allow founders to forecast outcomes with a level of detail and accuracy that was previously out of reach. Imagine receiving not only an Excel-based financial model but also a clear explanation of why AI generated specific projections. This level of insight enhances decision-making and ensures that financial plans align closely with strategic goals.

Training Your AI

Building an effective AI system requires investment, but the rewards are substantial. By training AI with your company's data—spreadsheets, presentations, documents, even videos—you create a proprietary model tailored to your operations. Over time, the prompts and processes you use to train your AI become your intellectual property, a unique asset that can enhance your company's valuation when it's time to sell.

Incorporating AI into your technology stack is not just about efficiency; it's also about positioning your business to scale intelligently and make data-driven decisions with confidence. Artificial intelligence offers competitive advantages that enable smart adopters to get a leg up against their competitors. For growth-stage founders, the combination of a best-of-breed approach and AI-powered tools can be a game-changer.

Ask our AI assistant questions about Finance for Founders
https://finforfounders.com/ai-assistant

In-House or Outsource?

One of the most important decisions a founder must make when upgrading their financial department is deciding *who* will do the work. The choice often comes down to two primary approaches: building the financial function in-house or outsourcing it to an external provider. Each option offers unique benefits and tradeoffs, and the right choice depends on the company's needs, growth stage, and resources. Let's investigate what each approach entails.

IN-HOUSE: BUILDING YOUR OWN FINANCIAL FUNCTION

Choosing to keep the financial function in-house means the company retains direct control over its financial processes. Typically, this involves hiring a consultant to install systems, establish best practices, and train existing staff. Once the groundwork is laid, the company takes ownership of ongoing activities.

This approach works best for founders who value control even if it comes with higher cost. If you are looking to upgrade the team and system you have in place, or you require more specialized systems, then this approach may be the way to go.

Benefits:

- **Knowledge Retention:** In-house staff builds expertise, ensuring the company develops internal capabilities over time.
- **Customization:** Processes and systems are tailored to the company's unique operations and workflows.
- **Control:** Direct oversight allows the company to adapt and refine processes as needs evolve.
- **Cultural Fit:** Employees embedded in the company's culture and values make decisions aligned with its objectives.

Drawbacks:

- **Higher Initial Costs:** Hiring, training, and consulting fees can create a significant upfront expense.
- **Resource Intensive:** Founders and internal teams may spend substantial time and effort managing the transition.
- **Scaling Challenges:** Rapid growth can strain internal resources unless the team expands alongside the business.

Example

A marketing agency founder hired a consultant to implement customized project management and financial tracking tools. The consultant trains the in-house staff, who apply this knowledge to manage client billing, budgeting, and time tracking. Over time, the staff's deeper understanding of these tools helps the company operate more efficiently and align with its specific client needs.

OUTSOURCE: PARTNERING WITH EXTERNAL EXPERTS

Outsourcing involves hiring an external provider to perform financial tasks, from daily accounting to strategic planning. These professionals may work remotely and part-time, yet they are part of the founder's team. This approach provides flexibility and access to expertise without the burden of full-time staffing.

Outsourcing works well for founders who don't have much of a financial system in place. Perhaps the books are a mess, and you want them cleaned up and functioning properly without too much of a commitment from you. Outsourcing can get you up and running with a great new system quickly.

Benefits:

- **Cost Efficiency:** More affordable than building a full-time in-house team, especially for functions requiring occasional oversight

- **Expertise and Connections:** Brings specialized knowledge and industry connections, often able to refer to other valuable providers (e.g., HR, payroll, banking)
- **Scalability:** Easy to adjust the level of service based on business growth or changing needs

Drawbacks:

- **Less Control:** Founders may have limited oversight of outsourced tasks, which can lead to misalignment.
- **Dependency on Provider:** If the provider faces disruptions, the company may experience operational setbacks.
- **Use of Providers Systems:** You may be asked to migrate your general ledger or other applications to the outsourced provider.

Example:

The same marketing agency founder engages a fractional CFO and their team to handle accounting, reporting, and financial planning. As the company grows, the founder hires a full-time CFO to join the management team while retaining the outsourced team for ongoing support. This blend of in-house and outsourced resources proves highly effective as the company scales.

CHOOSING THE RIGHT APPROACH

The decision to go in-house or outsource depends on priorities like cost, control, and your current stage of growth. Earlier stage companies tend to go with outsourcing because they are seeking a rapid upgrade and don't have much infrastructure in place. By understanding the tradeoffs, you can build a financial department that not only meets today's needs but also supports tomorrow's growth.

Build One Phase at a Time

Building a high-performing financial department in a growth-stage company is a phased approach. Each phase lays the foundation for the next, ensuring your financial operations evolve systematically, avoiding chaos and inefficiency.

PHASE 1: THE FOUNDATION — ACCOUNTING

Everything begins with accurate, timely, and accessible data. This is the Accounting pillar discussed in Chapter 4. It is the bedrock of a functioning financial department. Without reliable data, there's no hope of generating meaningful reports, actionable insights, or strategic advice.

If you're working with a limited budget, start here. For companies without prior professional financial management, the improvement can be dramatic—and achievable within as little as thirty days. A strong accounting system provides the clarity needed to scale.

PHASE 2: UNLOCK INSIGHTS — REPORTING

Once your accounting foundation is solid, the next step is Reporting (Chapter 5). Upgraded accounting systems feed better data into your reporting engine. Basic financial statements like your income statement, balance sheet, and cash flow statement become more reliable. Supporting schedules such as accounts receivable aging or sales reporting become tools for decision-making, not just compliance exercises.

From here, you can enrich your reporting with trend analysis, scorecards, variance reporting, and visually engaging charts. Many companies enhance this phase with third-party tools that integrate seamlessly with accounting software, giving them a reporting engine that informs deeper analysis and guides decision-making with clarity. These cloud-based tools are available today at a reasonable cost.

PHASE 3: PLANNING AND ANALYTICS

With solid data and reporting, you're equipped to take on Financial Planning and Analysis. This is where you map out the future—starting with an annual plan broken down by month. Projected financial statements give you the foresight to make informed decisions. Imagine the decisions you would make today if you could look into the future and see what actually happened.

Key performance indicators (KPIs) already used by management should be folded into this plan, with discussions on adding new, industry-relevant KPIs. Armed with reliable analytics, you're no longer just tracking the past but shaping the future.

> **FINSIGHT**
>
> **Learn which KPIs are important to investors in your industry and start tracking them.**

PHASE 4: THE PINNACLE — ADVISORY

The final phase is Advisory. When you've built a strong foundation with accounting, reporting, and analytics, your financial team—or external advisors—can use this data to shape their strategic insights that drive the Key Three objectives: more sales, profitability, and cash flow. This phase turns your financial department from a support function into a driver of growth that directly influences higher valuation.

By following this phased approach, you're not just building a financial department. You're creating a financial engine designed to scale alongside your business. Skipping phases can lead to costly missteps, but with a methodical plan, you'll gain the insights and confidence needed to grow your company with clarity and control.

ASSESSMENT: IMPLEMENTATION

Rate yourself on the following questions according to how satisfied you are with each. Insert a number between one and ten in each box and add them up. One means you are very dissatisfied; ten means you are very satisfied.

1. How clear are you on the specific improvements needed in your financial processes and controls to support your company's growth? _____

2. How confident are you in your ability to prioritize and implement financial changes without disrupting day-to-day operations? _____

3. How prepared are you to invest time and resources into upgrading your financial technology stack? _____

4. How familiar are you with the pros and cons of adopting a best-of-breed technology approach versus an ERP system? _____

5. How equipped do you feel to decide whether to keep financial operations in-house or outsource them? _____

6. How confident are you in identifying the right consultants, software, or outsourcing partners for your financial function? _____

7. How well do you understand the phased approach to upgrading your financial department, from building a foundation in accounting to achieving strategic advisory capabilities? _____

8. How willing are you to delegate responsibilities within your financial processes to ensure proper segregation of duties and scalability? _____

9. How aligned is your management team on the importance of financial upgrades and their role in implementing changes? _____

10. How prepared are you to embrace a continuous improvement mindset, knowing that upgrading your financial department is a phased and ongoing process? _____

Add up your score and write it here: _____

INTERPRETATION

Score Range: 10 to 60
Not Ready Yet

You may need to focus on foundational knowledge, alignment, and resources before tackling major financial upgrades.

Score Range: 61 to 80
Somewhat Ready

You have a moderate level of readiness but should address gaps in understanding, resources, or alignment before fully committing to change.

Score Range: 81 to 100
Fully Ready

You're well-positioned to implement changes effectively and can move forward with confidence.

Scan code to take the Implementation assessment online
https://finforfounders.com/implementation

10

Capitalizing Your Company

Lindsey sat nervously in her chair as she waited in the video conference waiting room. She knew she did something wrong. She hid something from people who trusted her. They will want to know why. She thought about how she was going to explain herself. She'd recognize the instant the other faces showed up whether her sin would be forgivable or not. She planned to calibrate her response accordingly.

The screen lit up with familiar faces. Mike, Elliott, Julien, and Troy. She studied Mike's face. If he was upset, he didn't seem to show it. He started the call with a smile, but no small talk. He got right to it. "So, Lindsey, Troy organized this call and gave us a little background. Why don't we start with you telling us what happened?"

She paused before speaking. Nobody seemed hurt or angry. Her first impression was that they were curious. Even Troy, who could get animated at times, seemed to be taking his cue from the serenity of Mike's team. Like many meetings before, they saw a problem and wanted to work through it with their no-nonsense approach. She noted the one thing she did not see. She did not see any judgment.

"It seems I got us in a bit of a pickle," Lindsey began. "But the truth of the matter is that I saw an opportunity and think it will ultimately pay off." She took a long pause. "I just underestimated what it would take to start and how long—and how much cash—it would take to get that payoff."

"This is your company, Lindsey." Mike jumped in first with a conciliatory tone. "Our job is not to tell you what you can and cannot do. Our job is to recommend to you different solutions and to help you balance the tradeoffs of each. It's important to us that you feel like you've been properly equipped with the information you need to make great decisions. Even if those decisions don't work out, and not all of them do, at least you can be confident that you made your choices with the best available information at that time."

"I appreciate that, Mike," Lindsey said with a sense of relief. She expected a lecture, although Mike had never delivered one to her before.

"Do you want to share with us why you chose to make this decision without our input, and why you waited so long to let us in?"

Mike was a skilled interrogator. The master of the open-ended question, he always knew how to concisely frame one that conveyed no judgment but immediately voiced the matter everyone wanted to address. By asking permission he was allowing her to decline to answer.

While Lindsey didn't want to answer, she knew she had to. She had to rebuild trust. "Look, Mike, I know the way I went about this was deceptive. This team has been great. You've transformed the way we work financially, and I've benefited greatly from your work. I also really enjoy working with all of you. And I trust you. So please know this has nothing to do with you or the confidence I have in this team.

"As I've gone down this journey of our little business 'growing up,' I realize that I'm starting to lose something. I feel like I'm losing control. Not logically, I know that what you have put in place has actually given me *more* control. But emotionally. I used to be able to make financial decisions without ever having to consult anybody. I can't do that anymore. I know I can't, I know I shouldn't, and I know why. I know these things. Yet I did what I did anyway."

Lindsey was surprised by how good it felt to get everything she had been experiencing off her chest and the words just kept flowing. "I think I did it because I wanted to assert some control back over my company. I have some issues around money and finances. Maybe it was the way I was raised. I didn't have much growing up. With what you've put in place, I'm starting to see more cash than I had ever seen before. I felt like it was burning a hole in my pocket.

"I've always had a passion for software. I thought if I could get this thing going on my own I could reveal to you something spectacular and that you'd all be on board with it. But I was afraid that if I came to you with this idea beforehand, this team would convince me not to do it. So rather than ask permission I decided I'd beg forgiveness. Which is what I am doing now."

Mike said, "Lindsey, thanks for sharing that and for being authentic. I know that was not easy for you."

"My pleasure," she replied.

"Our mission is to support your strategy to help you achieve your objectives of growing your sales, profit, and cash flow. If you felt strongly that this software would help you achieve your objectives, we'd do everything we could to support that effort. I think we've demonstrated a pretty good track record of that so far."

"You have."

"Good. You mentioned that this is an emotional issue for you. I've got some experiences I'm happy to share with you about that some other time. Would that interest you?"

Lindsey just remembered Mike was a founder, too. He works with other founders. This is why he was so calm. He's seen this before. He expected to hear something a lot like what she had to say. He'd have some great insights to help her work through her fears around money.

"I'd love that," she replied.

"Great, we'll get it on the calendar after this meeting. Now, let's talk about how we can attack the problem at hand."

Mike and Elliott asked additional questions about developing the software: customer needs, use cases, timelines, milestones, functionality, payments, and launch date. The call was nearing its end when Elliott chimed in with the next steps.

"Lindsey, this is a solvable problem," he said. "I'd like to take some time to develop a new set of projections to see what completing this project does to our capital base. If we need to raise additional capital, I'll come up with some options for you. I expect we'll be done in about a week."

Lindsey felt a wave of relief wash over her. There was a solution here. She didn't kill her company. Best of all, she didn't fracture her team. They were behind her and wanted to find the best solution, just as they always did. But there was one thing Elliott said that bothered her. It was something she'd never done before and never thought she wanted to do.

Raise capital?

* * *

Capitalizing your company means securing the money you need to run and grow your business. At its core, this is about ensuring your business has the cash to meet its obligations today while building toward its goals for tomorrow. After the initial startup funding from the founder, there are three primary sources of capital: internal cash flow, debt financing, and equity financing. Each has its own benefits, challenges, and implications for your business.

> **FINSIGHT**
>
> **After initial funding, the three sources of capital typically used by a founder are internal cash flow, debt, and equity.**

Internal cash flow is often the most desirable way to capitalize a company because it involves reinvesting profits back into the business. This approach keeps you in full control without the obligations of repaying a loan or diluting ownership. However, there's a catch: the business must be profitable for this to work.

If you're reinvesting profits, you're not taking those funds out as personal income, which can be a tough decision for some founders.

It can also take longer to achieve your exit objectives because internal cash flow arrives more slowly than a large debt or equity cash infusion. But for those who commit to this strategy, the long-term rewards can be substantial. Your company grows on its own earnings, and you maintain full control.

Debt financing is usually the first external option chosen by founders. Often this takes the form of a revolving line of credit at a bank, which provides flexible access to capital. Many founders get one when they start their companies. They draw on it as needed and repay it over time. For growth-stage businesses, this can be a lifeline to smooth out cash flow gaps or fund expansion projects. Debt brings its own risks: borrowing without a solid repayment plan or relying on debt to cover ongoing losses can lead to financial trouble down the road.

Equity financing involves selling to others a share of ownership in your company. This approach can bring in significant capital without adding debt to your balance sheet. It does not accrue interest, and you don't have to pay it back. But it's not without cost: when you bring on equity investors, you're not just sharing profits—you're also sharing decision-making power. The goal with equity financing is to create more value in the business so that everyone, including the founder, earns a return on investment when the company eventually has a liquidity event, such as the sale of the business. There will be pressure from your investors to pursue the best exit possible.

How you capitalize your company needs to be considered in the context of your company's ability to generate income and wealth over time for you personally. Income is what your business pays you now. It's the cash flow that supports your personal lifestyle. Wealth, on the other hand, is what you're building over time. This is the cash you expect to generate when you exit your business. The extent by which you invite others to share in your income and wealth needs to be considered as you evaluate your options.

Businesses fail for one reason: they run out of money before they've had a chance to prove their concept. You need enough runway to make the pivots all growing businesses make until they find the ones that work. That's why staying vigilant about your capital base and cash flow is critical. A misstep here could jeopardize everything you've built.

Internal Cash Flow

Internal cash flow is the lifeblood of your business. It's what remains after you deduct all expenses from your revenue. This isn't just a financial metric; it's a reflection of your company's health and ability to sustain itself without constantly seeking external financing. Strong internal cash flow means you can meet your obligations, invest in growth, and weather economic uncertainty. Conversely, weak cash flow can lead to stagnation, missed opportunities, or worse, financial distress.

One of the most valuable aspects of internal cash flow is its affordability. Unlike debt or equity financing, the only cost of internal cash flow is opportunity cost. What else could you have done with the money? For founders, this often boils down to a few key options: reinvesting in the business, setting aside funds in a bank account for future needs, or distributing profits back to the owners. Each choice has its trade-offs, and the right one depends on your company's growth stage, your personal financial needs, and your growth ambitions.

> **FINSIGHT**
>
> **Do not force your business to deliver more cash to you personally than it can produce.**

As a founder, you must generate enough internal cash flow to cover your personal expenses and reinvest in the business. If you can't, you'll face tough decisions about seeking external capital. Overdrawing from your business to fund personal needs not only slows growth but can also create tax complications. It's like milking a cow that's already underfed—eventually, the cow won't survive. On the flip side, underpaying yourself or failing to meet your own financial needs creates a different set of stresses that can distract you from effectively leading your company.

Relying solely on internal cash flow to fund growth has its limitations. While it's safe and ensures you retain full control of your business, it often means much slower scaling. For growth-stage companies looking to reach the next level, augmenting internal cash flow with external sources like debt or equity can provide the boost needed to seize opportunities more quickly. However, this strategy only works if the extra capital delivers a sufficient return. If you're borrowing money or giving up equity, it should be for investments that drive sales, profits, or cash flow significantly faster than you could achieve without it.

For founders, managing internal cash flow is about balance. Reinvesting enough to fuel growth, keeping enough to cover personal and business expenses, and avoiding the temptation to overdraw from the business are all critical. A disciplined approach to cash flow management can set your business up for long-term success, even if you occasionally turn to external funding to accelerate your journey. Remember, cash flow isn't just about survival—it's about ensuring your business thrives.

Debt Financing

Debt financing involves borrowing money that must be repaid over time, with the lender earning interest on the principal. For founders of growth-stage companies, debt can be a less risky option than giving up equity since it doesn't dilute ownership. However, it comes at a cost: the interest payments make debt more expensive than using internal cash flow. If you default, your lender could throw your company into bankruptcy.

TYPES OF DEBT FINANCING

Debt financing can be structured in various ways to meet different business needs. Here are the most common types:

1. Revolving Line of Credit

Revolving lines of credit are a favorite among founders. Much like a credit card, a line of credit provides access to a set amount of money that the business can draw from as needed. As long as the total balance stays within the credit limit, funds can be repaid and borrowed again.

This flexibility makes it ideal for short-term funding, such as launching a new project or financing receivables awaiting payment. Some banks require the loan to be fully paid off for at least thirty days each year to ensure it remains a short-term tool rather than a long-term liability.

2. Term Loan

A term loan provides a lump sum of cash up-front, which is repaid with regular principal and interest payments over the loan's term. This type of loan is often used for making large capital investments or funding long-term projects. It's useful when you seek stable fixed payments over a period of time. Some term loans feature a "balloon payment," where a substantial amount is due at the end of the term, allowing for smaller payments along the way.

You should consider using a term loan instead of a revolving line of credit when the funding need is for a long-term investment rather than a short-term or recurring expense.

3. Convertible Note

Convertible notes are a hybrid of debt and equity, often used in early-stage financing. They accrue interest like a traditional loan but convert into equity during a future financing round, typically at a discount to the next money in. This option is especially popular among startups planning to raise institutional capital and often appeals to individual investors in the company's initial stages.

KEY CONSIDERATIONS WHEN BORROWING

Personal Guarantees and Collateral
Most bank loans require personal guarantees and collateral. Be prepared to pledge assets or sign guarantees, which hold you personally responsible if the business cannot repay the loan.

Debt Service Calculations
Before borrowing, calculate your debt service—the total principal and interest payments due over the loan term. Ensure you borrow enough to meet your needs but not so much that servicing the debt strains your cash flow. You want your return on the investment to be higher than your cost of capital. So, if your annual interest rate is ten percent over ten years, you'll want more than an annual ten percent return over the same period.

Loan Underwriting
For larger loans, underwriting is an essential process where banks assess the risk of lending to your business. Be ready to provide financial statements, collateral, and insurance coverage. Banks often require compliance with covenants, such as maintaining certain financial ratios. Breaching these covenants can result in default, where the bank may demand immediate repayment.

If you are in default, you typically have three options:

1. Work with your current lender to cure the default.
2. Find another source of financing to repay the loan.
3. Seek the protections of bankruptcy court.

PREPARING TO BORROW
Presenting a clean balance sheet is crucial when approaching a bank for a loan. Lenders evaluate your company's liquidity, liabilities, and your personal financial standing. Key metrics include:

- **Debt-to-Income Ratio:** Monthly debt payments should not exceed thirty-five percent of gross monthly income.
- **Working Capital:** Current assets should comfortably exceed current liabilities.
- **Debt Service Coverage Ratio (DSCR):** Operating income should cover at least 120% of debt obligations.

By demonstrating financial stability and a clear repayment plan, you increase your chances of securing favorable loan terms.

Equity Financing

Equity financing is a method of raising capital by selling an ownership stake in your business. This could involve selling stock in a corporation or a partnership interest in an LLC or S-Corp. Unlike debt financing, which requires repayment with interest, equity financing allows a company to secure funds without a repayment requirement. It comes at a significant cost—giving up a portion of ownership and, with it, some control and profits. This is often more costly than debt when measured by future payoffs sacrificed by the founder to raise equity capital.

TYPES OF EQUITY: PARTNER EQUITY AND STOCK EQUITY

Equity financing can take two forms: partner equity and stock equity, each suited to specific business structures.

Partner Equity

In partnerships, such as LLCs or S-Corps, equity takes the form of contributions made by the partners. These contributions represent the initial and ongoing investment by the partners to fund the business. Over time, partner equity may decrease as partners take distributions from the company's earnings. This approach works well for entities where profits flow directly to the partners for tax purposes.

Stock Equity

Stock equity is the issuance of shares representing ownership in a corporation, typically a C-Corp. This type of equity includes common stock, which grants voting rights, and preferred stock, which often comes with specific dividend rights and priority over common shareholders during liquidation. Unlike partner equity, stock equity is not withdrawn directly from the company. Instead, shareholders realize their returns by selling their shares or receiving dividends. However, dividends are subject to double taxation—once at the corporate level and again as personal income (covered in Chapter 8, Taxes).

BALANCING RISK AND REWARD

Equity financing is inherently risky for investors because there is no guarantee they will be paid back. This is why they demand high returns to compensate for their exposure. However, this risk also comes with the potential for significant rewards if the company succeeds. For founders, equity financing provides a way to raise capital without the pressure of repayment, making it a flexible option for fueling growth.

THE COST OF EQUITY: HIGH STAKES AND DILUTION

Equity financing is often the most expensive form of capital. Investors expect a premium for the risk they take, which can come in the form of substantial ownership stakes. For founders, this means dilution—giving up a portion of your ownership, which could significantly reduce your share of the financial upside when the company is sold or goes public. In a partnership, selling equity means sharing future distributions, further impacting founders' long-term returns. You'll likely have to accept investors onto your Board of Directors, who will have a say in key business decisions.

Consider a simplified example of a founder who needs $1 million to grow his business. His business is worth $10 million today. He thinks he can sell it in five years for $20 million.

If he sold equity, a 10% stake is worth $1 million. If he sells five years later he's paid out total estimated distributions of around $500,000 to the investors, 10% of his profits over that time. This could be much higher based upon how profitable the company is. At exit he pays investors plus 10% of the purchase price: $2 million. Equity cost him $2.5 million.

If he borrowed that money instead at 10% he would have had a fixed interest expense of around $500,000 over the five years since he's not sharing profits. He would have repaid the $1 million principal at the exit. His total debt cost is $1.5 million.

The question the founder has to ask is whether removing the requirement to repay the $1 million raised was worth at least an additional $1 million it cost.

FOUNDERS' SKIN IN THE GAME

Founders are the first to invest equity in their business, demonstrating confidence in its potential. When seeking external investors, the level of founder equity is often scrutinized. Investors want to see that founders have significant "skin in the game" to ensure they are fully committed to the success of the venture. This equity contribution serves as a signal of dedication and alignment of interests between founders and investors.

Income Versus Wealth: Understanding the Difference

When building their companies, founders aim to maximize both their income and wealth. These two concepts are closely connected, yet they serve distinct purposes in a founder's financial journey. Understanding the difference—and how to strategically manage both—can significantly impact your business decisions and personal financial future.

INCOME: THE CASH YOUR COMPANY GENERATES

Income represents the cash flow your company produces, typically measured by EBITDA. This is a critical metric because it reflects your company's profitability and its ability to generate cash. That's why it's a key driver of valuation at exit. When your company generates a healthy EBITDA, you have choices about how to allocate the cash: keeping it for yourself, reinvesting in the business, or a combination of both.

For example, consider a founder whose company generates $8 million in revenue and $2 million in EBITDA. This founder might decide to take $1 million out of the business, using a portion of that to pay taxes on their net income. With the remaining cash, they have further options:

1. **Invest Outside the Business:** Placing some of the income into assets outside the company, such as public stocks or real estate. This diversifies risk, reducing over-reliance on the business for financial security. Investments in retirement accounts, for instance, can even offer tax advantages.

2. **Reinvest in the Business:** Using the remaining cash to fuel growth within the company can yield a strong return. If the company's EBITDA-to-revenue ratio is 25%, reinvesting $1 million could potentially generate $250,000 or more in additional EBITDA, strengthening both income and valuation.

WEALTH: THE VALUE YOU REALIZE AT EXIT

Wealth, on the other hand, is the culmination of your efforts—what you gain when you sell your business. This typically arrives as a lump sum, which might include future payouts based on deal terms. Your company's valuation at exit is generally a multiple of its EBITDA, meaning the income you've built over the years directly influences the wealth you realize upon sale.

A significant exit can be transformative, especially when combined with years of high income and strategic reinvestments in other wealth-building assets. This combination can lead to the creation of generational wealth. These are assets so substantial they require professional management and are designed to provide financial security for future generations.

Building for the Future

The interplay between income and wealth means founders must make careful choices throughout their journey. By balancing the need for immediate cash flow with strategic reinvestments and diversifying assets, you not only grow your business but also position yourself for a successful and rewarding exit. Whether your goal is to enjoy the fruits of your labor now or to create a legacy for generations, understanding these dynamics is key to maximizing the financial impact of your hard work.

ASSESSMENT: CAPITALIZATION

Rate yourself on the following questions according to how satisfied you are with each. Insert a number between one and ten in each box and add them up. One means you are very dissatisfied; ten means you are very satisfied.

1. How well do you understand the concept of internal cash flow and its role in capitalizing your business? _____

2. How confident are you in your ability to balance reinvesting profits back into the business versus meeting personal income needs? _____

3. How effectively do you evaluate whether taking on debt financing is a better option than using internal cash flow for business needs? _____

4. How well do you understand the risks and benefits of different types of debt financing, such as revolving lines of credit and term loans? _____

5. To what extent do you consider the trade-offs between maintaining full ownership and giving up equity when seeking capital? _____

6. How knowledgeable are you about the implications of equity financing on your control of the business, profit-sharing, and long-term wealth creation? _____

7. How effectively do you balance decisions to maximize current income versus building wealth for a future business exit? _____

8. How confident are you in your ability to evaluate whether external financing (debt or equity) will generate sufficient return on investment for your business? _____

9. How well do you understand the interplay between income (cash flow) and wealth (long-term value) in the context of capitalizing your business? _____

10. How satisfied are you with your overall understanding of what capitalizing your business means and how it impacts both your business growth and personal financial goals? _____

Add up your score and write it here: _____

INTERPRETATION

Score Range: 10 to 60
Needs Immediate Focus

Your understanding of business capitalization is limited. Consider dedicating time to learning more about internal cash flow, debt, equity, and the balance between income and wealth to ensure your business is well-capitalized for growth.

Score Range: 61 to 80
Improving Understanding

You have a foundational understanding of how to capitalize your business but could benefit from deeper insights into how different methods impact your income and wealth generation.

Score Range: 80 to 100
Capitalization Savvy

You have a strong grasp of capitalization principles and how they contribute to maximizing your income and wealth. Focus on refining your strategies to align with your long-term business goals.

Scan code to take the Capitalization assessment online
https://finforfounders.com/capitalization

12

The Payoff

It had been two years since Lindsey started to fund her software project. Her instincts were correct. While development took a bit longer than expected, and was more expensive, the app was a hit. She developed a tech-enabled service offering that added a new recurring revenue service line for her company. It opened up a large new market for her. Recurring revenue now accounted for twenty-five percent of her overall revenue and was growing fast.

Lindsey arrived at the table to see Mike already seated. They didn't see each other as much as they used to when they first started working together almost three years ago. He had become a good friend and eagerly accepted her offer for lunch. She had something she wanted to discuss with him.

"Mike, the difference between where my business is now and when your team joined is remarkable to me. We're now doing eight-figure revenue, my profits have never been higher, and we are growing strong. I'm thinking ahead and want to ask you: when should I start thinking about selling this business?"

Mike smiled and said, "Right now. You can never start too early. The first thing to do is to get proper representation on the deal. Doing it yourself rarely leads to the outcome you want."

Lindsey thought back to her interactions with Hal. She basically represented herself then. Repeating that debacle was exactly what she wanted to avoid.

"I have somebody I'd like to introduce to you who could help you figure this out," said Mike.

"Oh," Lindsey said, a bit confused. "I thought you did that."

Mike continued, "Your financial team's role in a sale is to help you close a deal on favorable valuation and terms for you. There's a lot of work your financial department has to do above and beyond their regular work. To get the right buyer and negotiate the best deal for you requires a skilled dealmaker. That's not us. You need a Mergers and Acquisitions (M&A) advisor who focuses on helping founders like you sell their company. An investment banker."

"Okay," said Lindsey. "Let's set up a meeting."

"You got it. His name is Matthew and you'll love him. He's straightforward, personable, and has a ton of experience representing companies like yours."

* * *

Lindsey clicked the link in her invite. Mike and a new face immediately appeared on her screen. Mike began the meeting. "Lindsey, I'd like you to meet Matthew." After hearing about his background and exchanging a few pleasantries, Matthew got to work.

"Lindsey, I understand you tried to sell your company once before without any luck. I know you are eager to avoid that happening again. If you don't mind, I have a little deck I like to share with founders to help set expectations about what's to come in the sale of their company."

"Sure. I'd love to see it."

"I'd like to start by talking about your potential buyer. There are three things I want to cover." Matthew put up a slide on his shared desktop:

POTENTIAL BUYERS

- Who they are
- What makes a seller attractive to them
- How they operate

"There are two types of buyers," Matthew said. "Strategic and Financial."

STRATEGIC VERSUS FINANCIAL BUYER

Matthew popped a chart up on the screen and started talking about the differences between the types of buyers.

Aspect	Strategic Buyer	Financial Buyer
Who they are	Companies in the same or related industry looking to complement their current operations	Private equity groups, investment firms or individual investors looking for a return on investment (ROI)
Motivation	Create synergies to enhance operations, market position, or growth. An example is acquiring a new product line.	They want to buy, grow, and eventually sell the business for a profit.
Valuation approach	Typically willing to pay a higher price (a "strategic premium") because they value the synergies they expect to realize after the acquisition.	Focused on current and projected cash flow (e.g., EBITDA) and ROI rather than synergies—less likely to pay a premium
Post-sale plan	• May integrate your business into their existing operations • Might retain some or all your staff but could reorganize or eliminate redundant roles • Typically less focused on keeping the seller involved long-term unless your expertise is critical to the transition	• Often keep the current management team in place to run the business • May invest in the business to increase its value. • Typically holds the business for three-to-seven years before selling it to someone else or going public
Price	Likely to offer a higher price due to synergies	May offer a lower price focused on financial performance
Involvement post-sale	Typically less focus on keeping the seller involved long-term unless expertise is critical—this is because they already know how to run a business like yours.	Often want the seller to stay involved, especially in management. They don't know how to run your business like a strategic partner would.
Impact on business	May significantly change the business or its culture to fit its own	Likely to invest in growth and maintain the current culture

He then went on to elaborate further. "Strategic buyers look for companies that complement their current operations. Financial buyers are looking for a return on their investment. One buyer is not 'better' than the other. Understanding their perspectives will help you make some decisions about where you think you will get the best deal as well as what happens after the deal closes."

Matthew saw Lindsey nodding and moved his cursor to the column on the right. "For a strategic buyer, your company eventually will be absorbed into the buyer's company where it could remain for a very long time. This buyer's perspective is much more long-term than the financial buyer's. The financial buyer will try to sell your company again to someone else, for a much larger profit. This could be as soon as a few years after the close. These are things to consider as you decide which deal is right for you. Do you have any questions?"

Lindsey responded, "How does a founder decide which one to pursue?"

Matthew replied, "We don't really choose them as much as we let the market choose us. If we are evaluating offers from each, then we'll have conversations about what happens post-close. We'll evaluate those tradeoffs versus price and work from there."

"Got it," said Lindsey.

WHAT MAKES A COMPANY ATTRACTIVE TO A BUYER

"There are many things that make a company attractive to a buyer," Matthew explained. "The top two in every deal is the ability of the company to generate cash and the quality of its management team. Without a compelling rationale for both, it's hard to convince a buyer to pay top dollar for your company. In my experience, founders have anywhere from an over-inflated to an unrealistic view of what their business is worth. They think about what it is worth to them—not to the buyer." Matthew paused to let the concept sink in.

"Savvy buyers know this," he continued. "They'll make an offer with a tantalizing valuation only to pair it with terms that make realizing that value almost impossible. Would anybody think they won a $10 million lottery if the payout was $1 a year for ten million years? Of course not. The point is that terms matter as much as valuation, and in many cases are even more important. Any deal we do for you has to have terms that get to an acceptable cash number for you to receive at exit. So, to get that valuation up at acceptable terms, let's look at what the buyer first evaluates when they start to get to know a company—generating cash."

Strong EBITDA: The Yardstick that Measures Financial Performance

Matthew continued, "Buyers are very focused on EBITDA because it measures the ability of the company to generate profitable cash flow from its operations. It removes certain accounting items like interest, taxes, and depreciation that result from operations, but does not drive it. Purchase prices are determined by applying a multiple to EBITDA. There are other valuation methods that may be used to support the price, such as discounting the future cash flow of your company, but the EBITDA multiple is the most common. The multiple is determined by the market: what other buyers paying for companies similar to yours? The multiple can change based upon market conditions."

"Can you give me an example?" asked Lindsey.

"Sure," Matthew said. "A company showing $1 million of EBITDA in an industry where buyers are currently paying six times EBITDA will get a valuation of $6 million."

"So, if I have a number in mind, for each additional dollar of EBITDA I could generate an additional six dollars of valuation?"

"Exactly."

Lindsey hadn't thought of that before. Now she knew what adding value meant to her company. She made a note to herself to ask Mike to update her reports with multiples to her EBITDA so she could track growth of her company's valuation.

"Any other questions?" asked Matthew.

"Not for now. Please continue," replied Lindsey.

Matthew returned to the deck. "Buyers want to know the quality of your EBITDA. Earnings is driven by revenue and they want to see increasing demand for your business. This is why so many buyers love recurring revenue and pay a premium for it. It is more predictable and scalable. Reliably increasing revenue in any business requires building a commercial sales engine. For professional services firms like yours it's a bit trickier as the founder is usually responsible for bringing in the business. That's a risk for a buyer. They prefer sales that do not require a founder to close."

That statement resonated with Lindsey. She felt she was still too close to the sales process. She made a mental note to address that while Matthew continued.

"In the initial stages of screening opportunities, buyers will apply the 'Rule of 40'. You may have heard of this before. Most buyers use a simple formula. Take your average annual percentage growth rate of sales and add to it the EBITDA percentage of annual net revenue. So, if you have a three-year average annual revenue growth of 20% and your last twelve months EBITDA is 20% of your net revenue, then you've achieved 40%. Understand?"

"20% annual revenue growth plus 20% EBITDA % equals 40%. Got it." Lindsey noted.

> **FINSIGHT**
>
> Buyers often use the Rule of 40 in the initial stages of evaluating a company to determine if they want to take the next step.

"Good. It's a quick test for a buyer to see you are growing both revenue and profit at the same time. These are the companies they are willing to pay a premium for. Plenty of deals get done that are not 'Rule of 40' but they usually don't fetch a premium valuation and terms. To get that premium, buyers want to know that your business can operate profitably at scale. They want to know the way you deliver your product and services, and the support structures in place to ensure that delivery, are effectively managed so their productivity increases continuously over time. This is where the management team comes in. Once an acquisition candidate passes the Rule of 40 test, focus quickly shifts to the management team."

Matthew flipped to the next slide.

Strong Management Team

"We all know that a strong management team is required for strong financial performance. Have you ever asked why it's particularly important to a buyer?" Matthew asked Lindsey.

"I just figured it's like you said—you need strong performers to have strong performance."

"True, but there is another problem for the buyer. Buyers don't like to see a business too dependent on its founder. What happens to the business if something happens to them? That's too much risk, so the buyer will look to see a strong number two in place and key roles in operations and sales filled with strong performers. Now, if the buyer has concerns about the founder's impact on future performance, they will introduce terms to make sure the founder stays around long enough to make the acquisition pay off. This is where earn-outs come in. The buyer will pay out the valuation you negotiate over time. It will be tied to certain performance metrics. If you don't meet them, you don't get paid. Sellers hate earn-outs, and they can be avoided if the buyer believes that management can carry the company to the next level, with or without the founder. Make sense?"

"I get it," said Lindsey as she made a note to herself. *Get a #2 in place.*

"Now we know who the buyers are and what they are looking for. Let's talk about how they operate."

HOW BUYERS OPERATE

Matthew resumed, "The buyer of your company will be much better at purchasing your company than you will ever be at selling it."

This was intriguing to Lindsey. She leaned into her monitor a little more.

Matthew explained, "Buyers evaluate hundreds of opportunities a year and close very few of them. An entrepreneur sells their business only once. Sure, some serial entrepreneurs do more but they will never close as many deals in their career as a professional M&A person will close in a single year. People who have chosen a career in M&A are skilled at negotiating price and terms in their favor. They've been trained at it and have perfected it during every deal that they do. They are transaction folks whose primary objective is to acquire companies at the best price and terms to them. They negotiate down what the founder wants to negotiate up. The buyer and seller are fundamentally conflicted.

"Financial buyers in particular have to be aggressive on price and terms. It's fair to say they have more pressure on them than a strategic buyer. The cash they are using to purchase your business has come from investors who believe they can earn a high return on their investment. They have both a fiduciary responsibility to them as well as a strong performance motive. If they can't demonstrate a strong return on investment track record, they can't raise new funds for new acquisitions. They would go out of business quickly if this were the case.

"The deal pipeline is the lifeblood of the buyer's business. What you should realize is that you are competing with a whole lot of companies like yours. You have to position yourself as the worthiest candidate."

Matthew paused his presentation. "We've covered a lot, Lindsey. Do you have any questions?"

"Just one," she said. "What kinds of earn-outs have you seen before?"

"For companies that were not very well prepared, or who had no choice but to sell, anywhere from 60% to 100% of the deal."

"Wow! You mean people will do a deal with no cash at the close and hope they get paid? Who would agree to that?"

"People who have no choice," Matthew replied.

"Let's make sure that's not us," said Lindsey

"That's why firms like mine exist!" Matthew said. "I think this would be a pretty good time to share with you how we work."

WORKING WITH AN M&A ADVISOR

Matthew put another slide up on the shared desktop summarizing how his firm works:

WORKING WITH AN M&A ADVISOR

- Complete market assessment
- Source potential buyers
- Negotiate letter of intent (LOI)
- Assist due diligence
- Negotiate definitive agreement
- Fees
- Next steps

Complete Market Assessment

Matthew explained what a market assessment is and why it's the first thing they do.

"We'll start the project to see what the appetite is for acquiring companies like yours. The survey we prepare is based on deals recently completed in your industry. We subscribe to a database with proprietary deal information, so we'll share with you what we found. It answers the question as to if now is a good time to sell. While great companies always get sold, it always helps to have favorable market conditions. Our report will also include a range of valuations for your company and potential deal terms. It's a starting point to set expectations. Based on that assessment, you can decide if you want to move forward."

Source Potential Buyers

"We want to appeal to both strategic and financial buyers," said Matthew. "We'll do this through an auction process which will create demand for your company by inviting multiple prospective buyers to submit a bid. As bids are prepared, we'll lay out for you each one side by side so you can compare price and terms. An auction process also has a psychological benefit. If buyers know multiple people are possibly bidding for a company, it makes the company more attractive to a buyer. Buyers don't like to miss out on good deals.

"When we evaluate a deal, we always look at it from the perspective of how much cash you will likely walk away with. Terms matter. During these conversations we spend a lot of time with founders on the valuation. A lot of folks are fixated on a number. Maybe it's ego or bragging rights, I don't know. But it's a problem because if the buyer senses the seller is fixated on it, they will offer a high valuation at difficult terms.

"A few years ago, I worked with a business owner who insisted upon a $10 million valuation. It was a family business, and he wanted to brag about how much he sold it for. The owner was a big talker. This became a problem especially when I was counseling a more restrained approach. During due diligence, the buyer got less comfortable with the risk and adjusted for it by making practically the entire deal conditional on an earn-out. I didn't like the deal and urged him to walk away, but he insisted on closing.

"We closed and I never heard from him again. Then, three years later I ran into him. He looked very different, certainly much older. He confessed the total he received from the deal was about $2 million and he had to go back to work. 'I should have followed your advice,' he said, 'but my ego got in the way.' It was hard to see him like that."

Mike spoke up for the first time. "I don't think you're going to have that problem with Lindsey. One thing I've learned is that she is very pragmatic. She's also coachable."

"That's great to hear," Matthew said. "I find that founders who approach a deal with an open mind and flexibility have the best outcomes.

"So, we have offers, now we have to negotiate them to arrive at the letter of intent you want to sign."

Negotiate Letter of Intent

"Choosing the right one for you is based on a few things. First, we define your goals. How much cash do you want up front? What would you settle for after the close, if anything? What role do you want to have after the acquisition? There are several goals we'll have to figure out.

"Next, we'll analyze the financial and non-financial terms of each offer. We'll help you evaluate the tradeoffs of each and how they align with your goals. We'll start to narrow down the list and focus on those that work best for you.

"After that, we'll consult with your transaction attorney to get their legal review of each LOI and engage with the prospective buyers on any changes. Once that's done, we'll negotiate the final LOI for you to sign.

"That's the process. Here's a couple key things to take away."

A Letter of Intent is Not the Final Deal

Matthew took a sip of water before speaking. "First, the LOI is indicative of the transaction the buyer is willing to close pending the outcome of due diligence. It's a stake in the ground; however, it could change dramatically during due diligence and the negotiation of the final agreement.

"At this point, Lindsey, you would need to retain a lawyer to assist with the LOI. This person should also negotiate the definitive agreement since they would already be familiar with the LOI. I can recommend some attorneys who specialize in transactions like yours. I cannot emphasize how important it is that you have the right lawyer on this deal. They are trained to reduce risk as low as possible for their clients. Some overdo it and can turn off an investor. This is why you need a lawyer who specializes in transactions. They know the give and take. They also know how to be responsive and keep the deal moving. Time delays can kill a deal. They are aware of the current market because they are doing deals. They may even know the buyer's attorney which could be useful. Lots of reasons to get the right attorney."

"Makes sense," agreed Lindsey. "Please send me the names and I'll make some calls."

"Will do," replied Matthew.

FINSIGHT

Keep the process moving. Time delays can kill deals.

Assist Due Diligence

Matthew moved to the next topic at hand. "We'll be helping you get through due diligence. This is a thorough check up of your business before a buyer closes the deal to purchase your company. It's the buyer's way to make sure everything is as presented and there are no surprises. Here I would rely on Mike's team to take the lead in setting up the Virtual Data Room (VDR), collecting the necessary data, reviewing it, and populating the data room."

Negotiate Definitive Agreement

"Your attorney is responsible for drafting the agreement and negotiating various legalities," Matthew said. "I will be helping that person with the business terms of the deal. First, I'll make sure the deal structure and terms are suitable for you and align with the expectations from the LOI. We'll put reasonable protections in place for you and work through your employment agreement and transition terms. There are a host of other things, but the most important is that I'll be guiding you through to the close.

"I've found as due diligence wraps up and a closing date is in sight, the vibe of the deal changes for the seller. The reality of some big changes in their life starts to set in, not the least of which is the cash that's about to change hands. This is also when the deal can get fragile. The buyer is making a big commitment as well and wants to make sure they have examined everything and that they are comfortable. Both sides have a lot invested in the process at this point. This is also where the biggest surprises seem to happen. Maybe a small detail got missed or maybe the company's performance has deteriorated from the focus on due diligence. Whatever the cause, the important thing to realize is that as the deal nears its close, surprises can have a really big impact. So, it's important to minimize them by keeping the buyers fully informed every step of the way."

"Got it," said Lindsey.

"Great," responded Matthew. "Any questions before I move on?"

"Looks like you're about to address it. What does this cost?"

Matthew smiled and said, "Let's talk about that."

M&A Advisor Fees

"Okay, we've stepped through the various activities we'll do for you, how they work and why we're doing them. Here's how our fees work."

Lindsey stiffened a bit. She knew this would not be cheap.

Matthew put up a slide:

M&A ADVISOR FEES

- $50,000 upfront retainer
- Success fees
  - 5% of the first $1 million EV
  - 4% of the next $1 million EV
  - 3% of the next $1 million EV
  - 2% of the next $1 million EV
  - 1% of any amounts beyond $4 million EV
- Example: $10 million deal = $250,000 fee

"Firms like mine charge two fees for transactions like this. One is a non-refundable retainer. This ensures the commitment of the seller and covers our costs of marketing the deal. This is a one-time upfront payment of $50,000."

He paused for a second to let Lindsey absorb the number. "The next part is a success fee. We are only paid this if we close the deal for you. This fee is paid in cash on closing day out of the proceeds from the deal.

"We use the Lehman Formula. Some folks call it '5-4-3-2-1.' The formula applies a certain percentage based on the size of the transaction. The percentages change based upon breaks in the deal value. There's a 5% fee on the first $1 million of deal value, then 4% for the next $1 million, and so on until a flat fee of 1% is applied to amounts $4 million and above.

"The size of the transaction, its price, is also referred to as Enterprise Value (EV). About half the firms like mine use this formula. For example, an enterprise value of $10 million results in a fee equal to 2.5% of the deal: $250,000. That's a retainer of $50,000 and success fees of $200,000. We'll calculate your fees after we do a market survey and see what your enterprise value could be."

Before Lindsey could react, Mike stepped in. "Lindsey, you'll also have to pay for the work we do for you during due diligence, as well as the attorney costs. This could add at least another $100,000 or so to your cost. That amount is variable because we charge for our time, so more time leads to more cost for you."

Lindsey's eyes grew wide, and she backed slightly away from the camera, as if recoiling from it. Based on her ideas of her company's value, she'd estimated she would be paying more in fees than she earned just a few years ago! She'd also be paying over $100,000 fees even if the deal did not close: Matthew's retainer, Mike's due diligence support, and legal fees.

"Wow!" she said. "I knew closing deals like this are not cheap, but these numbers take my breath away!" She smiled. She knew she was going to pay it. It was the cost of avoiding a big mistake she swore never to make again.

Matthew responded very calmly to her reaction. Clearly this was not the first time he had gotten a reaction like this. "Let me explain to you why firms like mine price deals this way.

"First, it aligns our interests. We make more money when we make you more money.

"Second, smaller deals require just as much work as large deals, especially when the seller may be less sophisticated. This is why it's harder to find investment bankers for smaller deals—they can earn much more by doing bigger deals. You're competing with other deals for an advisor's time.

"Third, smaller deals have a greater risk of not closing. Closing is how we make our money. We price in a premium for taking that risk.

"Finally, complexity matters. We don't know how complex a deal is going to be when we get started, so we price this in."

Matthew wrapped up by saying, "If I am doing my job, the fee will not impact what you eventually get out of this deal, because it will be so much higher than what you are thinking now. Speaking of which, what would be a good payout for you, Lindsey?"

"My last prospective buyer offered me $6 million with $3 million cash up front." She wanted much more than that now.

Matthew smiled. "With what I know so far, I'm confident we can do much better for you. We just need to properly prepare you."

"I was hoping to hear that," Lindsey responded.

"I thought you would! Let's talk about next steps."

Next Steps

Matthew flipped to a slide and began, "First, I'm going to put everything we discussed into writing for you. I'll send that to you in a few days. Then you're going to decide two things: do you want to move forward with a sale now and do you want to do it with us? If the answer is yes to both, we'll send you a contract for your signature. We'll schedule a kickoff meeting and begin the process."

"Sounds good. One final thing before we go. How can I best position my company to secure a premium deal?"

Mike replied, "Boost your revenue growth and EBITDA percentage as best you can. Demonstrate your growth is not only sustainable but increasing. Make sure you have a clearly defined number two and solid management team in place. There are plenty of other things around your customers, services, etc., that will matter greatly, but profit and the management team are the most important."

"Anything else I'm missing?" Lindsey asked.

"Actually, yes. I was just reading an article the other day that I think you'll find interesting. I'll send it to you, but I want to share with you a snapshot of a chart in it."

He spoke while searching for the chart. "It's a listing of avoidable mistakes that kill deals. About seventy percent of failed exits are diligence related."

8 AVOIDABLE MISTAKES THAT DERAIL DEALS

1. Cleanliness and integrity of financials
2. Lack of formal exit planning
3. Caginess during due diligence
4. Lack of familiarity with numbers
5. Losing focus on business performance
6. Running a too narrow process
7. Not pre-defining ideal outcome
8. Letting emotions cloud judgement

Source: Exit Ready Magazine, Vol. 1 2024 Edition, Axial

Matthew talked through the chart briefly and promised to send her a link. "Let's get a meeting on the calendar in two weeks after you've had a chance to review our plan." They agreed to a date and signed off the call.

Lindsey let out a heavy sigh. She had a lot to think about.

Scan code to download Matthew's presentation
https://finforfounders.com/slide-deck

* * *

Lindsey launched her video conferencing app and was the first one on. Matthew and Mike jumped on shortly. "Well," Matthew began, "what did you think of our last meeting?"

"It was very informative," Lindsey began. "You certainly gave me a lot to think about! Where I landed is that I don't think we are quite ready. But when we are, you are the one I want to lead this process."

"Sounds good!" Matthew said, then followed up with a question. "Why don't you think you're ready?"

"To start with, I don't have a number two. I've long thought about installing one. Now I've got a reason to do so. There are a couple of high performers on my team I think could be perfect for the role. I want to start a process of developing them to see which one could someday become CEO.

"Next, I think we can do more to boost our sales growth and margins. Mike's team has helped tremendously with that. We've recently launched a service line based upon an app we developed that has taken our business in a new direction. It's a recurring revenue model showing a lot of promise. I'd like to give that more time to develop.

"I'm also too involved in the sales process. I want to find a way to completely remove myself from it. This has been on my mind for a while, and I think I've been unwilling to step back because I love to sell. Whenever we had cash flow problems before, that was how I solved it. I know that it won't work for a buyer willing to pay me a premium. I have to change that, and now I have a reason to.

"Finally, I want to spend some time preparing to sell. It's a great focusing event to get us to improve our valuation. Even if we don't sell we should be generating more cash so that we can invest in even more growth. There's a mindset shift and a bit of a cultural shift that needs to happen. I think we're better served taking a little time to develop that."

"Lindsey, this sounds like a great plan. I have no doubt that when you are ready to sell you'll be very happy with the outcome."

"Do you think the market will be strong when it's time to sell? I don't want to miss out if you think we should be selling now."

"The market certainly matters," Matthew said, "but great companies can always get a great deal in a sale. I think it will be there for you when you are ready. If it's not, you'll be generating enough cash where you can wait until the market is more favorable to you."

"I'm glad to hear that," said Lindsey. "I'll be sure to keep you updated."

"Please do," replied Matthew.

Starting the Exit Process

Lindsey spotted Rachel at a high top on the deck. Two glasses of water sat in front of her. Lindsey settled into the empty seat across from Rachel. Rolling waves washed ashore a few yards away. Lindsey could see why Rachel picked this place. The view, gentle breeze and sweet, salty air was immediately relaxing.

They ordered cocktails and a couple small appetizer plates. The conversation began with the latest happenings in their personal lives. When the food arrived, the talk turned to business. Rachel kicked it off. "Well, I know you've been busy, because you've rescheduled this three times! At least you waited until we had better weather," she joked.

"Yes, life has been hectic, but it is settling down a bit. And it has been extremely productive."

"Tell me," said Rachel.

"It all started with that meeting I had early last year. The one with Mike and Matthew I told you about. Matthew gave me some advice on things I could do to make my company more attractive to a buyer willing to pay a premium price. It made sense to me, and it was going to be a lot of work as well as investment. So, we got started and a funny thing happened."

"What happened?"

"Well, our financial performance really picked up. Like, dramatically. I knew the payoff could be in what I would make in the sale.

What I didn't expect was how focusing on the sale would make our operations so much more effective and efficient *during* our sale preparations. Our sales are the highest they have ever been, and I've never made more money."

"How much?" Rachel asked.

Lindsey was taken aback by the bluntness of the question. They had shared many private things before, but money was not one of them.

"You mean how much am I earning?"

"Yes. You don't have to give me a specific number. But I am eager to see how far you've come. A few years ago, you complained that you were working very hard but never felt like you were earning enough to compensate you for your efforts. You were stuck in that for a while. Now it seems like you've broken out of it. I've been with you since you started this business and have been rooting for you the entire time. I ask because I want to celebrate what you've achieved and—I won't lie—I'm a bit curious."

"Well, let's just say I'm at least an order of magnitude better than where I was a few years ago," Lindsey admitted. Rachel was sharp and could do her own math. Lindsey was earning well over $2 million a year from the business she created.

"That's awesome!" said Rachel. They clinked glasses.

"How did you do it?" she asked.

"The first thing I did was commit to finding a strong number two who could run this business. I had to get out of my own way and focus on developing new business and developing talent. I couldn't do it while still sitting in sales calls, approving proposals, and doing a million other things that somebody else could do better than me. One weekend I wrote down every task I did, and it ran to over a hundred items. I knew it had to change.

"I had a couple high performers on my staff I thought could take on the role. I gave them various assignments to see which one would be the best fit. After about six months, I gave one a Chief Operating

Officer role and the other VP of Sales. I recently elevated the COO to President and made the sales VP an Executive VP. They both seem really happy in their roles because their performance is outstanding.

"Their impact on the business was immediate. The sales VP went about creating a commercial sales engine. This new system cut me completely out of the sales loop. I focused more on speaking at events, networking, and promoting the business. My role in developing and approving proposals, as well as meeting with prospects, was over. We have a deal desk now and a process to ensure only qualified prospects were offered proposals that would be profitable. With me out of their way, lead generation and close rates improved dramatically. I think not having me part of that process really liberated them. They felt free to hit their sales targets and our sales leader was a great motivator for them.

"The President installed new systems to ensure top-notch customer satisfaction. She did it by developing a talent management plan to source, hire, and train our people. She created career development plans so people could see a path to their own professional growth. Overlaying it all is a compensation plan based on sharing our profits. Everyone loved it. And started making more money.

"Now I get to spend my time on strategic matters. My work is different. I used to dread meetings because they'd always lead to more work for me… reviewing proposals, creating spreadsheets, etc. Now I'm delegating, deciding, and having more meaningful conversations about how to develop this business. I'm also taking more time off.

"It was hard for me to let go of some of these things. But by doing so I think I empowered people to unlock new levels of problem-solving and innovation I thought only I could do. It's been so gratifying to see others share the same passion I have for our work."

"Wow, Lindsey, that is amazing. I'm so proud of you!"

"Thank you," Lindsey blushed. "That means a lot to me."

"You ready to sell?"

"I am," Lindsey replied.

* * *

"It's great to see you again, Lindsey," said Matthew. "Mike has told me that you've made great progress since we spoke last year."

"I think we have," said Lindsey. "I reached out to see if this is the right time to begin our sale process."

"It could be," replied Matthew. "Why don't you give me an update?"

"Sure. Let me start by saying that our meeting last year had a profound impact on me. You gave me a very clear roadmap of what to do to get a premium price for my company. It helped that Mike and his team did a masterful job helping me implement our plan and develop metrics to track and measure our progress. So, thank you for that."

"My pleasure!" said a beaming Matthew.

"I started with your recommendations about the management team. I now have a President and EVP of sales established. We have other key management roles focused on service delivery, customer satisfaction, and marketing. They've been doing a great job.

"I tasked my sales EVP with building a commercial sales engine that excludes me. He did that and the results speak for themselves. Our three-year average annual sales growth is around 35%. The highest gains came in the last year and are expected to grow in the coming years.

"We really focused on building our EBITDA. The new service line leads the way—recurring revenue is nearly 50% of our business and is our fastest growing segment. It is also highly profitable. Our trailing twelve-months EBITDA percentage of net sales is 27% and we expect it to be north of 30% in a year."

Matthew noticed she was rattling off metrics like a pro. Knowing her numbers this well was bound to impress buyers. He did a quick Rule of 40 calculation before speaking.

"Lindsey, that is wonderful news. Looks like your Rule of 40 is 62, which is very strong. The market for companies like yours has gone into a bit of a lull over the past year but it is picking up. Great companies get great deals, and you have a great company. I think we should do a market analysis for you and get back to you with some valuation ranges and possible terms. If you like what you see we can engage and kick off the process. Sound good?"

"Sounds great!" Lindsey exclaimed.

"Terrific," Matthew said. "I'm very excited to start working on this project with you. There's a little story I like to share with founders as they start this journey. Mind if I share it with you?"

They had some time left on the call. "Sure," said Lindsey.

"It's very important to understand the perspective of the buyers you'll be speaking with. They are transactional. It is in their nature to get a great deal. Most founders are builders. It is in their nature to build a great company they fall in love with. There is a philosophical disconnect between builders and dealmakers. Understanding this will help you greatly during this process."

"*Okayyy,*" said Lindsey, dragging out the word. *Where is he going with this?* she wondered.

"Do you know the parable of the scorpion and the tortoise?" asked Matthew.

"No."

"A tortoise is about to swim across a river when a scorpion appears and asks to cross the river with him by riding on his back. The tortoise refuses because he is afraid the scorpion will sting him while he is swimming.

"The scorpion replies that if he were to sting the tortoise while swimming, they both would drown. Seeing the logic, the tortoise gives the scorpion a ride on his back. Halfway across the river, far beyond the point of no return, the scorpion stings the tortoise.

"As they begin to sink, the tortoise asks why the scorpion stung him as now they will both surely die. The scorpion replies, 'Because it is in my nature to do so.'"

"I think I know what you are getting at," nodded Lindsey.

"Don't let a scorpion get on your back," said Matthew. The call ended.

Lindsey had a reflective moment in front of her blank screen. She looked around her office, a place she had been coming to for years without any thought. She noticed small details she hadn't noticed before—as if she were creating a memory of an important place she may not visit again.

All this is going to change. Everything is going to change, she thought.

Hal popped into her mind and she felt a brief pang of anxiety. She felt so much shame after that experience. Could this experience be even worse? Her business is different now in every way since then. She knows that. Still, what if she were wrong? No outcome is certain. What if all this time and effort resulted in an outcome even worse than Hal's? So much was at stake.

Am I really ready for this? she thought to herself.

* * *

Lindsey developed her business to be appealing to buyers because she chose to do so. She met with an M&A expert who knows what buyers are looking for and she followed his advice. Selling a business is never an accident. The best valuation and terms come from following a deliberate path. A great result should be expected after great preparations have been made.

> **FINSIGHT**
>
> Getting a premium valuation and terms should be expected when great preparations have been made.

Here are a few of the key things Lindsey did in her preparations:

- She engaged a reputable advisor and listened to him.
- She emotionally prepared herself for a sale. The buyer is getting a deal they can close.
- She addressed the key areas of importance to the buyer: growing demand and increasing profitability. This maximizes valuation and terms.

There are some other things Lindsey could do to prepare for a sale and communicate that she is serious about selling:

- Perform a background check on herself
- Get a review or audit of financial statements prepared by a reputable CPA firm
- Get Quality of Earnings report

These things are not required and can be costly. Having them prepared sends a strong signal to the buyer that you are serious about a sale.

Background Check

The buyer will likely run a background check on the founder and maybe the executive team. Run one on yourself to see what comes up. If there is any adverse information, you can address it with your deal team ahead of time so you can manage buyer expectations.

Financial Review or Audit

Some founders have their annual financial statements reviewed or audited by an independent accounting firm. They tend to be useful in larger deals. It may save some time during due diligence as the independent audit verifies numbers the buyer would otherwise have to verify themselves.

If you go this route, make sure to engage a reputable firm that is known to potential buyers. Having your small tax preparer prepare an audit will not carry the same weight with the buyer and you'll have wasted your money.

> **FINSIGHT**
>
> **If you get an independent review or audit of your financials, be sure to engage a reputable accounting firm.**

Quality of Earnings Report (QOE)

A Quality of Earnings report is a detailed analysis of a company's earnings to determine how sustainable, reliable, and repeatable they are. It gives the buyer confidence in the company's profitability and cash flow. Like an audit, they are prepared by independent accountants. They are expensive and will become outdated as the business grows. So, if you choose this route, you'll need a recent QOE for your deal.

Buyers may do their own QOE and will not rely on those prepared for sellers. Even so, a seller-prepared QOE can help a seller:

1. It is an indication that the seller understands buyer concerns and is collecting data to address those concerns.

2. It provides another data point to help negotiations. You can use the QOE to give you some negotiating leverage.

3. Not many smaller deals have a QOE, so you'll stand out among the deals that buyers screen.

4. It is useful to you as you can see how a buyer would potentially view your business. You can address any deficiencies with your deal team beforehand.

Getting Letters of Intent

The sale process kickoff call had all the key players on it: Lindsey, her President, her financial team of Mike, Elliott, Troy, and Julien and their M&A advisor Matthew. Matthew started the call.

"Okay, folks, we're here today to kick off our sale process. We have a lot to cover. Typically, we start by naming the project. When we communicate, it gives us context and keeps things confidential. It's better to say, 'Project X' instead of "We're selling the company.' Anybody have any ideas?"

They bandied about some names. Nothing seemed suitable. Then Troy piped up, "How about Project Phoenix?"

"Why Phoenix?" asked Lindsey.

"Well, this whole thing started by that awful experience you had with Hal. You've led a lot of changes that I know will result in the sale you want. So, it's like Phoenix rising from the ashes."

"I love it!" Lindsey exclaimed. Project Phoenix was born.

* * *

Over the next hour or so, they hammered out a plan.

1. **Lindsey would identify an internal team to assist with due diligence.**

   She would tell them candidly that she planned to sell the business. She made sure each member of the team would participate financially in the deal if they were still employed with her when the deal closed. She wanted to make sure there was continuity in sales and service delivery. When it appeared the deal was going to imminently close, Lindsey would announce to the rest of the company what was happening.

2. **She would get an audit and Seller's Quality of Earnings.**

   As her fiscal year was almost over, she'd get an independent audit of her financials and a seller's QoE. While expensive, this would give potential buyers comfort in her numbers. She was not going to make the same mistake twice. She suspected not many other companies her size would have both. This could differentiate her company among the hundreds of deals multiple buyers would be evaluating.

3. **The team would prepare a data room.**

   Matthew provided them with a due diligence checklist used by buyers. Her team would start assembling the documents needed for it.

4. **Matthew would prepare a Confidential Information Memorandum (CIM).**

   He would identify a list of target acquirers and circulate the CIM among them. His goal is to collect multiple Letters of

Intent. He'd lead the negotiations for each and help Lindsey select the best one for her. While Matthew was working the CIM, Lindsey would engage a transaction attorney.

5. **After signing the LOI, pass due diligence and close the deal.**

   Matthew warned that this is the time in every deal when things get intense. Even though they are well-prepared, due diligence is a grind. Everything happens with a sense of urgency and that can be wearying. The important thing is for everyone to stay focused, be responsive, and prepare to answer the same questions more than once. This is where a lot of emotions come into play, because people are working very hard and there is a lot of money on the line. The most important thing, Matthew said, was to make sure the business did not suffer at all during due diligence.

The team agreed they would go to the market around the second quarter. By that time, they will have had a track record for how the year began, and if they were at or ahead of their plan, it would be positive news to prospective buyers. It also aligned with a pickup in deals in her industry. It seemed the market currently was very favorable to companies like hers.

The plan was in place. The team was excited. The only thing left was for Lindsey to give her final approval.

This was a pivotal moment for her. She stood at the crossroads of desire and doubt, questioning if this deal was truly what she wanted. Everything would change after this moment. Closing this deal meant leaving a life behind. The routines, work, relationships, everything she had done for years, would be different. She'd be working for someone else, following their rules. She loved living life on her own terms and wasn't sure how she'd give that up. Change never came easy for her and this was a big one. Her biggest ever.

Besides, the outcome was far from certain. Deals are filled with big ups and downs. This was not going to be easy. Once word got out she was trying to sell, she'd be wearing that label until she actually sold her business. Her team might feel that she no longer wanted to be their leader. What impact would this sale have on them?

On the other hand, Lindsey was always a risk taker. An exceptionally clear thinker, she loved the challenge of figuring things out. She thought about her life if she chose not to sell. She had a good business, but at some point, it would struggle to grow. It needed new people, customers, and capital to become what she thought it could be, even if it grew without her. She did not want a lifestyle business. There was no acceptable alternative to selling her company.

Her choice was crystal clear. She would move forward and accept whatever came her way. Things had a habit of working out for her, even when the outcome was murky at the start. Things would work out again.

She gave her approval. The meeting ended and her team got to work.

* * *

Lindsey finished lunch at her desk after the monthly management meeting with Elliott wrapped up. It was clear they were having a spectacular year. They exceeded every meaningful sales and profit metric.

Her biggest concern was keeping up with high demand. Project Phoenix was progressing nicely. The data room was set up and populated. Matthew had completed his CIM and was circulating it. In a few minutes they would meet to discuss his progress.

Matthew's face appeared on her monitor. It was just he and Lindsey on the call. He was smiling.

"Why do you look like you have some good news?" Lindsey inquired.

"Because I do, and I have an interesting story to share as well."

"Do tell!" said Lindsey curiously.

"Turns out Hal got wind that you were selling," Matthew said. "When he heard you were represented, he reached out to me instead of calling you directly. He figured you'd just refer him to me given what happened last time."

"He's right," Lindsey stated flatly.

"So, I sent him a CIM. He called me back a few hours later. He bowed out—said there was no way he could afford an acquisition this size! He was impressed with your progress and wished us good luck. He mentioned he might reach out to you at some point to congratulate you on all you've accomplished."

Lindsey thought about this for a minute. Part of her was still angry at Hal for making her feel so ashamed. They had not spoken since her deal with Hal fell through. The reality is that there is no way she'd be in the position she's in today if Hal had not been so harsh. He was the spark that led to these changes. She decided she'd be gracious.

"I'll reach out to him."

"I'm sure he'd love to hear from you," Matthew encouraged.

"So, now for some more good news. We've got four very motivated buyers. I'm going to start to schedule meetings among them, you, and your team. We'll need to set up data rooms for each to give them information they need to prepare their LOIs. Things are going to get pretty intense for you for the next couple months. Think you're ready for it?" Matthew smiled.

"Very much so!" Lindsey beamed.

* * *

Matthew was right. It was intense. Each meeting led to requests for more information, a meeting to walk through the info, then more info requests, then another meeting. Multiplied by four investors. One dropped out. Another got added. The entire time the team had to drop what they were doing to respond. She worried her business would suffer.

Except the business didn't suffer. The systems they had built were able to withstand the additional pressures brought on by Project Phoenix. People were working more for sure. Too many nights and weekends were interrupted. But they were getting all their work done.

After two months, Matthew started getting LOIs. He signaled to the market that he had received offers and set a deadline to move along the laggards. Matthew contacted Lindsey just after the deadline had passed. He had four LOIs. His team was going to review each one and get back to her with their findings. In the meantime, he was going to email them over to her.

"How do they look?" she asked.

"I think you'll be very happy. It's clear to me there's a good deal for you here. The challenge now is figuring out which one is the best path to a great outcome for you."

After some back and forth with Matthew, Lindsey's attorney, Elliott, the buyers, and the buyer's attorneys, she eventually settled on an LOI and signed it. She felt relieved and excited. Another gate passed through. *I hope I made the right choice,* she thought to herself after submitting her e-signature.

* * *

Lindsey was able to get four LOIs because she spent time and money making her company attractive to buyers. She made a deliberate decision to invest in growth and to scale her company. She took a risk—there was no certainty when she made the decision to sell that things would work out. By putting in financial guardrails to measure and track key performance indicators, she had valuable information telling her whether her risk was paying off.

Getting multiple-term sheets is a rarity, but it is possible if you are prepared. That means being well-represented by a skilled M&A advisor who can run the process. It means assembling a team that can manage the distractions of a sale process while also running a business. It means having your financial house in order. Due to their preparation and professionalism, her company was so far able to avoid the avoidable mistakes Matthew shared at their first meeting.

Lindsey knew that to obtain a big reward, she'd have to take a big risk. The valuation even on the lowest LOI was eye-popping to her. She never thought she'd ever have that much money. She didn't, yet. But someone thought her company was worth that much. It was very satisfying to her, and very empowering. The market was telling her she had a very valuable business.

All that was left was to pass due diligence, and close the deal. While most accepted LOIs lead to a close, they don't always close at the value and terms initially offered. Every LOI is conditional: only after completing due diligence and memorializing the definitive agreement will the final value and terms get settled.

Passing Due Diligence

Lindsey chose a deal with a financial buyer—a private equity (PE) firm well-known in her industry.

All the offers Lindsey received were strong in their own ways. The planning she did beforehand clarified what she wanted to achieve at closing and beyond. It made her final selection so much easier. The LOI negotiations went more smoothly than she expected. She was feeling very good about her choice.

As she should. It was a good deal. Solid valuation. Lots of cash at the close and a two-year employment contract while her firm transitioned to new ownership. Lindsey and her President would be kept on to run the firm as a "platform company."

A platform company is used to acquire other companies with the intent of selling the larger entity in a few years. The platform company's strategy, processes, and approach are applied to the companies they acquire. Offering this to Lindsey validates the confidence they have in her firm to scale rapidly. She would be expected to roll some of the proceeds she gets from the sale into equity in the new company (an "equity roll").

Matthew had said that getting the LOI was just the start of a laborious process. Due diligence was going to be much harder. Lindsey's team got off to a great start by populating their data room. Now that they had the buyer's checklist, they realized they were going to need to get a lot more data. Some of it was dynamic, like financial data that changes each month. Other data was obscure, like certain incorporation documents she thought they already had in their internal data room. Mike and his team would need to do a lot of sleuthing to get all this information pulled together.

THE DUE DILIGENCE CHECKLIST

At the start of due diligence, the buyer provided a checklist in a spreadsheet. These checklists differ by buyer, but they generally ask for this information:

1. Financial
2. Legal
3. Sales and Marketing
4. Human Resources
5. Information Technology
6. Suppliers (for companies with inventory)

Scan code to download a sample due diligence checklist
https://finforfounders.com/due-diligence-checklist

Financial

This section provides data on financial statements and all supporting schedules used to prepare them. The investor wants to make sure the financials they relied on to prepare their LOI is valid. They will also ask questions about budgeting and planning process, taxes, assets owned, debt owed, and a host of other questions.

Since financial data is dynamic—financial statements are prepared every month—be prepared to update this data throughout the due diligence process. The buyer will want the latest set of monthly financials for inclusion in the definitive purchase agreement. The day before the close the buyer may ask for a balance sheet updated through that day.

Legal

All legal matters are disclosed in this section, which is scrutinized just as closely as the financials. The buyer wants to ensure that any agreements made before closing are acceptable to them (and can be reasonably modified if they are not). They also want to verify that the contracts you claim to have signed, such as customer purchase agreements, are actually valid.

This area typically includes:

- Organization and Corporate Structure
- Material agreements
- Litigation
- Regulatory matters / compliance
- Intellectual Property Rights
- M&A activity

Sales and Marketing

The buyer is purchasing your company based upon its ability to deliver sales growth. Among other things, they will want to know your customer lists, how you generate leads, what metrics you track to convert new sales, how your sales team is structured and compensated, and how your commercial sales engine will perform in the future.

Things that give comfort to a buyer in this area are recurring revenue and long-term contracts. If these are absent from your company, you'll use the data you provide in this section to make your case that your business will generate demand at least as well as you projected it would when you signed your LOI.

Employees / HR

The most valuable asset you're offering to a buyer is your people. Their ability to perform in their new environment is critical to ensuring your business thrives under new ownership.

Your buyer is going to want to see how your workforce is structured. They want to know who they are getting and how their current employment with you fits into what they offer their employees. This section will provide data on:

- Employees roles, responsibilities, compensation, tenure
- Policies and procedures, like reimbursements and time off
- Employee benefits
- Organization chart
- Any employee grievances or actions currently underway or settled.

Information Technology

IT is a core function of every organization. If you've developed proprietary technology, they will address those questions in their Intellectual Property requests as part of Legal due diligence. What they want to know in this section is how you use technology in your business.

Be prepared to respond to requests about your current tech infrastructure (hardware, support), the cybersecurity controls you have in place, and a listing of the applications you currently use. They want to understand if there is any risk as well as to see if there is any redundancy in their tech stack that they can eliminate post-close.

Suppliers

For companies with inventory, the buyer will want to understand your supply chain and cost structure. They will want a listing of major suppliers, how you manage logistics, the cost system used for your products, and how you manage inventory.

MAINTAINING THE DATA ROOM

Keeping the virtual data room well-organized makes the due diligence process work much more effectively. Passing so many files back and forth ultimately leads to avoidable mistakes. Too many deals get complicated when an internal document is inadvertently uploaded to the data room or file versions are not properly controlled. A clean data room makes it easier for the buyer and demonstrates that your team is attentive to the details that are important to them.

Here are some things you can do to maintain a clean data room:

1. **Use the due diligence list provided by the buyer as your filing system.**
   These lists are often organized into the sections we discussed earlier in this chapter. Map out the folder structure in your data room to this list.

2. **Create a separate folder in your root directory for each section heading on the list.**
   Take the list headings and set up corresponding folders. Prepend each heading with a sequential number or letter so you can maintain the same order as the list you were provided. For example, if the first section is Sales & Marketing then create a folder called "A-Sales & Marketing." This way it will appear before "Financials."

3. **Give each file a unique ID that corresponds to its request.**
   Your request list will likely be numbered. Take the number
   for a request you fulfill and start your file name with it.
   When the list is sorted, the file names should appear in the
   order they appear on the list.

   If you must submit a batch of files (say, a year's worth
   of bank statements), put those into a single folder and
   prepend your file name with it. For example, request #6 in
   Financials to submit all bank statements becomes a folder
   called "6-Bank Statements." This way you don't have to
   spend time changing all the filenames.

   You will be expected to cross-reference the files you
   upload to your due diligence list each time you submit
   documents. Doing it this way allows you to easily copy and
   paste the filename to your document.

4. **Maintain a separate internal data room.**
   Create the exact same data room structure for a room
   you will use to prepare your responses. Clearly label it
   INTERNAL so everyone knows it is only for your team's use.

   Any files that are meant for internal use should
   be flagged as internal both in the filename and in the
   document itself. For extra security, protect the file with a
   password. Just don't forget the password. Microsoft Excel is
   very unforgiving when it comes to password protected files!

5. **Maintain a "finalized" data room.**
   This data room is also maintained only for your internal
   team. It has the exact same structure as the other data
   rooms. Its purpose is to stage files that have been prepared
   and are ready for final review before being uploaded to the
   buyer's data room.

   This helps with version control. When a file is in
   its final form, upload it to this data room. By virtually

segregating files that are to be uploaded to the investor data room, you greatly reduce the risk of including a file you did not want to include.

When other team members review and approve these finalized files, cut and paste them to the buyer's data room. This will remove them from the finalized data room, always keeping it empty until finalized documents have been put in it. You have the originals, and any supporting data, already in your internal data room.

6. **Submit an updated due diligence checklist with each submission.**

    As you populate the data room you should keep the due diligence checklist updated. This includes any clarifying information, filenames and locations, date of submission, and status. You can apply filters to this list to show only the data you are submitting on that day. Batch your submissions no more than once per day so you can better track them. Delivering in batches makes it easier for everybody.

7. **Never email files that belong in a data room.**

    Don't email any files that belong in the data room. You'll lose the ability to track them and may cause issues with version control. Email apps are terrible document management systems. It is better to upload the file and send people a link to it so they can be assured they have the correct version of a document.

MANAGING THE DUE DILIGENCE EFFORT

Due diligence pulls key team members away from their day-to-day responsibilities, jeopardizing the company's performance at a critical time. The best way to manage this disruption is to do what Lindsey did: prepare. By being "due-diligence-ready" you can minimize the disruption.

Even the most prepared teams will experience frustration and fatigue at some point. It's the role of the founder to recognize when this is happening and to take steps to take the pressure off. This means keeping a cool head when others are losing theirs. It may mean pushing back a deliverable to ensure a high-quality submission, or an unexpected day off for a team member. By staying focused and in control, you can minimize the chaos, maintain business momentum, and project confidence to potential buyers.

Closing the Deal

Elliott led the weekly internal due diligence status call, as he had been doing for the past several months. He began with an update of the latest investor requests, which have now numbered over one hundred since the start of due diligence.

"This is really starting to piss me off," Lindsey said with exasperation. The grind of due diligence was clearly wearing on her. "I feel like we've already covered this. Is there no end to these requests?"

"I wish it were different, Lindsey, but this is how the process works." While Elliott tried to hide it, clearly, he was getting frustrated, too.

"Is this typical, though?" asked Lindsey. "I mean, do all the deals you've worked on track like this one?"

"Too many of them do, I'm afraid," replied Elliott. "But I will say, this one seems to be taking a bit longer and their requests seem much more detailed than similar deals I've worked on."

"I guess the only thing we can do is to keep doing what we've been doing: continue to respond quickly to their requests with good data and walk them through it when needed.

"I'm afraid that's the best we can do for now," said Elliott.

It was not Elliott's fault. The team's responsiveness was excellent. Lindsey was getting angry with the buyer. After uploading a batch of documents to the virtual data room, the investor would often go quiet, sometimes for as long as a week. Then they'd call a meeting, ask a bunch of questions, and demand more data. This was starting to cause a lot of rework for her team, especially when it came to refreshing financial data that always changed. The buyer often asked the same questions over and over again.

The good news was that due diligence wasn't having any negative impact on her business at all. In some respects, it seemed to energize people. The monthly close meeting they had earlier in the week was nothing but good news. Year-to-date revenue and EBITDA were ahead of projections, as they had been since the start of the year. The forward momentum of the business could not be questioned. It was so good that Lindsey began wondering if she started this process a little too early. Would waiting until later this year have resulted in an even better deal? She pushed those thoughts aside. She made her choice with good reason, unless the buyer gave her a bad reason.

The buyer was about to give her a bad reason.

* * *

After that call with Elliott, the deal started to move a little faster. A new Managing Director, Chad, was brought in by the buyer to move the deal along. Definitive documents were being drafted, and the due diligence requests were slowing down. The past couple weeks saw some real progress being made, although a close date had yet to be discussed.

It was a late summer Friday afternoon and Lindsey's thoughts drifted to her plans for the weekend. She was wiped out and looking forward to emptying her mind at the beach. Her phone pinged. Matthew sent a text asking if she was free to meet with the buyer's team at 2:00 p.m. today.

"Sounds ominous," she texted back. She'd gotten texts like this before.

"Let's not worry about anything unless we have something to worry about. We'll let them speak first then respond. Okay?"

"Okay."

She clicked her link just before 2:00. The buyer's team got on the call at 2:05.

Chad got right to the point, "Lindsey, we've discovered something that has made us uncomfortable." He launched into a discussion about inconsistencies in customer contracts, the timing of revenue recognition was off, and a litany of other items that she thought were settled long ago. She listened, hiding her mounting anger behind a cool façade.

He wrapped up with the point of his meeting. "As a result, we need to reevaluate our pricing to take into account this additional risk."

"What are you saying to me?" Lindsey asked.

"We are saying that we are going to adjust your valuation downward. We'd also like to build some additional protections for us into our agreement." Chad started talking about what those would be.

Lindsey recognized this exactly for what it is. A negotiating tactic. Matthew had warned her about this. Late in a deal, sellers get fatigued. They just want to close. Buyers know this. Sometimes they introduce something unwelcome that the seller would have rejected earlier but accepts now just to get the deal done and move on. For some reason it always seems to happen on Friday afternoons. Like today.

FINSIGHT

Beware of this trap. Buyers may introduce unwelcome terms late in a deal. Fatigued founders too often agree with something that costs them just to get a deal done.

What Chad didn't know was that Lindsey was prepared for this. She thought through this exact scenario so many times since her awful experience with Hal.

She knew a scorpion was trying to hitch a ride on her back.

In the middle of Chad's diatribe Lindsey interrupted him "Chad, I'm going to stop you right there," she said curtly.

Chad had a quizzical look on his face. He wasn't used to founders speaking to him this way. He stopped talking.

"Before you continue you need to know three things," she said icily.

"First, according to our most recent monthly financial review, we continue to outperform our revenue and EBITDA projections—we are far beyond what we said we would do in our CIM.

"Second, we have complied with your every request. We've been thorough and responsive. Your own team has complimented us on how well-prepared we are for due diligence. We've demonstrated good faith throughout this process. Right now, I'm not feeling that our good faith is being reciprocated.

"Finally, I had three other offers besides yours and I chose your company." The implication in that statement was clear.

Lindsey continued, "So, when you tell me you have concerns then I must tell you that I have concerns as well.

"My biggest concern is our continued strong financial performance. We've shared with you our numbers and they speak for themselves. The fact that we are beating our projections accrues a bigger financial benefit to you than to me, because after the close, this great financial performance will be yours. I have not asked for an upward revision to the purchase price. You are trying to make a great deal for you even better by taking something away from me.

"I'm also concerned that I am hearing about this now. If you were even thinking about this being a problem, why didn't you bring it to me sooner? You've told us you appreciate how transparent we've been with you. Now I'm feeling our transparency is not being reciprocated by you.

"So, I am wondering what other surprises are in store for me before the close. Or, even worse, after the close.

"Here is what I am going to do. I know I can't shop this deal since you have exclusivity. I can't talk to the other prospective buyers who gave us LOIs. But I can terminate this deal, and I am now considering that. I am instructing my team to do no further work until I have decided if I want to continue following through on it. You'll be hearing from me early next week when I make my decision."

She paused for effect, staring blankly into her screen. Chad was speechless, eyes wider and mouth slightly open. His team looked around sheepishly, clearly uncomfortable. Matthew cracked just the slightest smile. Nobody said a word.

"This call is over," Lindsey said before snapping off her camera.

Her phone immediately rang. Matthew. She picked it up and said, "What just happened?"

"What happened was you shook a scorpion off your back, stomped it, then ran over it when you drove away!"

Lindsey snickered at the scorpion reference. That story landed well with her. "I'd love to know what's going on over there right now," she responded.

"We're going to find out soon. Let me handle this next step. I think right now it's best to let me carry the message. That's one of the benefits of having an intermediary—to work through conflicts. I just need to know one thing. Are you really ready to walk away? There's a lot of cash at stake."

"Without any hesitation, whatsoever," Lindsey stated. "I will not accept a deal that does not work for me, even if we are scheduled to close in an hour. I know what we are worth, and I am determined to get it. Worst case, I make more money over the next few years and sell at a higher valuation. And one more thing you should know... the reason why I don't play poker is that everyone knows I don't bluff."

Matthew said, "Very well. I'll get back to you as soon as I know more. For now, radio silence, even if they try to contact you. Okay?"

"Okay." They both hung up.

A wave of anxiety washed over her. *Did she just kill the deal?* Matthew didn't seem to think so or he would have said something. Was he in damage control mode or did he sense something else was up?

* * *

Lindsey felt remarkably serene after speaking with Matthew. She understood the value of the hard work put in over the years to make her company attractive to a buyer. She was absolutely prepared to walk away from any deal that did not work for her, no matter how near a closing they were or how much cash was at stake. In her mind, she just walked away from life-changing money and the deal was over. While she decided early in the process what her boundaries would be, following through on that decision was incredibly difficult.

In every deal there will be a "moment of truth" for a founder. It's a point where they learn of a term they don't like, a change in price, or something that materially alters their expectations during the deal. When this happens, you must figure out what is very important to you—then have the conviction to follow through on whatever it is you decide.

Lindsey risked an awful lot of cash and introduced tremendous uncertainty. She knew "big risks lead to big rewards" so was willing to take a big risk. She managed that risk, however, because her business was over-performing. There were other companies she had passed over who might be interested in re-engaging. Worst case, she'd continue operating the company for a few more years. She was earning more than ever before and that was only going to increase.

There was one other trick up her sleeve. Something Matthew had said to her earlier that she was counting on. It was the only thing buyers hated more than losing money on a deal. It's missing out on a great deal. The FOMO effect was real, and she knew she had a good company somebody would want to buy. She sensed this could be at play here.

She approached this process with clear-eyed confidence. Through her prior experiences she knew that even the best plans could go astray. She recalled an old saying, *"Plans are worthless, but planning is everything."* She was prepared for a situation like this and had considered her options before taking the risk she took. Her response to Chad was not impulsive. She had rehearsed her response many times in her head. Things had a way of always working out for her. This would, too.

She didn't have to work too hard to convince herself that the action she took was best for her and her company. Anxiety intruded anyway. Did she do right by her team? Some of them stood to make a lot of money and take their careers in exciting new directions. Matthew collected his fee at closing—he would lose that. Had she been a little too decisive too quickly?

Her thoughts moved to continuing with her company and saving the sale for another day. She was at peace with it, although the next few days would be turbulent as she ended due diligence and resumed running her business.

Besides, there's no way the buyer would engage now after the way she just treated them. *Would they?*

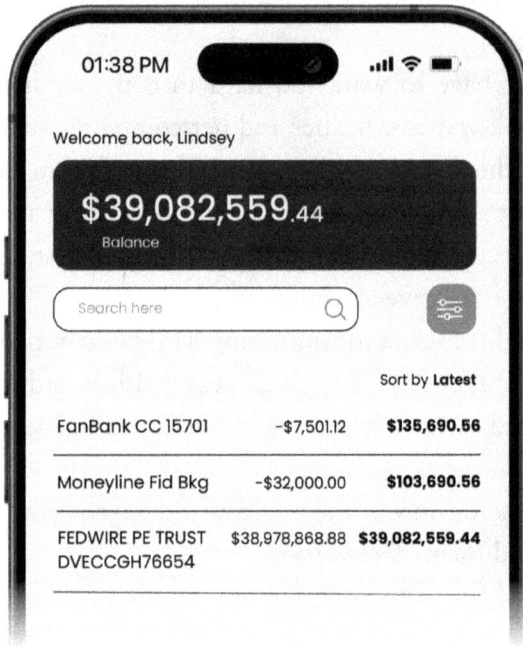

01:38 PM

Welcome back, Lindsey

$39,082,559.44
Balance

Search here

Sort by **Latest**

FanBank CC 15701	−$7,501.12	**$135,690.56**
Moneyline Fid Bkg	−$32,000.00	**$103,690.56**
FEDWIRE PE TRUST DVECCGH76654	$38,978,868.88	**$39,082,559.44**

* * *

Lindsey had been checking her phone every five minutes since the last e-signature was submitted a couple hours ago. Everyone told her it was on its way. Still, she would not believe it until she saw it.

Then it arrived. The wire transfer.

At first it didn't really register with her. She felt the same. She had meetings to attend, calls to make. The world had not changed much, but her world had. That was *so much money*. She went about her rather ordinary day, feeling very accomplished but focused on what she needed to do now.

Late in the afternoon there was a gentle knock on her open door frame. Mike. Holding a bottle of something, just smiling. The person who started her on this journey. That's when it hit her—everything was about to change. Seeing Mike brought it all rushing to the surface: the journey, the stress, the anxiety, the countless sacrifices, the relentless hours. She had achieved what so many chase but so few capture. She knew how rare this was. For just a brief moment, in front of Mike, she let the weight of it all wash over her—the triumph, the relief, the sheer magnitude of what she had done.

She composed herself quickly and hugged him before they sat down.

"Sorry, that's a little embarrassing," Lindsey said from behind a tissue. She sat down heavily in her chair.

Mike gave her a reassuring nod as he settled into the couch across from her desk. "Lindsey, this is completely normal. Every founder I've worked with in this situation has felt the same way. You're not alone in this. You've accomplished something that so few founders ever do. I mean, three weeks ago I wasn't sure this was going to happen!"

"Me either," Lindsey agreed. "But I felt strongly that a deal would happen."

"Good thinking," Mike said.

They rehashed what went down. Shortly after the meeting, Phil, the CEO of the private equity firm, heard the deal was put on hold by the seller. He demanded to see the video of the meeting.

He did not like what he saw. His team had been regularly informing him that the deal was gliding toward a close. Transition plans were underway. He had spoken with some board members about its potential. He knew this was a good deal; his firm was committed to it and he was not about to lose it. He was quick to get on the phone with Matthew to see what could be done.

Matthew called Lindsey after he spoke with Phil. Phil wanted to know if the deal was really dead or if it could be salvaged. The video of Lindsey's response to Chad impressed him. "Anyone willing to fight that hard for her company is going to be fighting that hard for our company. That's exactly what I am trying to bring to our team." He said he knew talent like that did not come cheap, leaving the door open for Matthew to modify the deal in Lindsey's favor. Phil needed an answer by the end of that day.

On their call Lindsey and Matthew agreed to ask for three things. More cash at the close. More equity for her equity roll without putting up more cash for it. A firm close date. They settled the terms over the next few days. As a sweetener, Phil removed Chad from her deal. "He's good," said Phil "but he's a bit overzealous. I needed to send a message to him anyway."

Mike shook his head chuckling while she retold the story. "This is a new one for me," he confessed. "But you definitely earned it. I've been doing this a long time and I don't think I've ever seen anyone so prepared, and so effective, at selling her company. You should be very proud of what you've accomplished."

"I am. Very much so. And I wouldn't be here without you. I'm deeply grateful for you putting me on this journey and supporting me throughout it," Lindsey admitted.

"So, what's next?" asked Mike.

"I guess, anything I want it to be," said Lindsey.

* * *

While not all stories will end like Lindsey's, in her case she did certain things that made it more likely to end with this outcome.

1. **Hired the right team of advisors**

    By working with professionals who knew how to conduct transactions, she filled a big gap in her own knowledge and skills. Having the right representation makes it far more likely you'll close a deal on the right terms and valuation.

    It will cost more, but the value they bring more than covers their cost. You can't get a deal done if you can't close it. You need closers on your team. Closing a sale of your business is very different from closing a sale of a new customer.

2. **Very coachable**

    Lindsey was very self-aware. She knew what she did not know. She was willing to try anything that seemed like it had a reasonable chance of working. She was curious, asking questions about the "why" as much as the "how." It was important that she had advisors who were also great coaches. She didn't have to be the owner of every idea. She was willing to let others have the spotlight.

3. **Managed risk**

    She relied on the expertise of her team and data to make sure she was on the right track. When the data suggested a course correction was needed, she did not hesitate to make those decisions, even when they were tough. Her advisors were great at advising her on various tradeoffs, so she was kept fully informed of the impact of her decisions.

Even with all this going for her, she still made mistakes. She went down the wrong path with her software idea and did it anyway even though she knew it was wrong. She was wise enough to pivot when her advisors told her it was not working and risk distracting her from her ultimate goal.

Lindsey's approach is pretty simple. Hire the right advisors. Make a plan. Execute the plan. Prepare for the unexpected. Pivot and move forward, applying your learnings along the way. Keep an open mind. The approach works and founders who follow it can enjoy the same spectacular outcome Lindsey realized.

Epilogue

Lindsey looked out the window, deep in thought. Soon she'd be doing something she long dreamed of. She rehearsed in her mind what she wanted to say for about the thousandth time. She wanted to make sure she delivered her message just right.

Earlier in the year she had retired from her new company after a four-year stint. She loved it more than she thought she would. Phil was very supportive, granting her new opportunities to develop her career and leadership skills. She was very much the public face of her company, which attracted new acquisitions that drove her company's growth.

She wound up with a great relationship with Chad. Turned out his negotiating skills came in handy as he was tucking in acquisitions for her team to manage. They had a great deal of respect for each other.

The sale of the platform company came a few years sooner than she expected. It was a gigantic windfall for her—even more than she got from her original sale. With generational wealth in hand, she formed a charitable foundation and got to work on her passion for philanthropy. She was so excited because today was the first time she was going to meet one of her foundation's beneficiaries.

The pilot opened the cabin door and released a short set of stairs. Lindsey descended down onto the hot, white tarmac. It was cold where she left from, so she basked in the warmth of the south Florida sun for a moment. Private air travel was one indulgence she allowed herself. She wanted to personally meet all the people she hoped to help with her new foundation.

She stepped into an air-conditioned black sedan and made the short trip to the school. She saw the name of her foundation on a banner hanging above the door. A small group met her warmly at the curb and escorted her into a room filled with young women.

It was the inaugural class of the center she donated to promote female entrepreneurship. She hoped to work with young minds to plant the seeds of the power of business ownership. Somewhere in this crowd, she hoped, was someone she could inspire to accomplish even more than what she did.

The dean of the school walked up to Lindsey to shake her hand. The crowd quieted. He said, "Everyone here is thrilled to meet you. I know the weather was a bit rough when you left. We're glad you arrived safely."

Lindsey paused and took in her surroundings. She saw the faces of eager future entrepreneurs, full of potential and ambition. All eyes were upon her.

"Indeed," she thought to herself, *"I have arrived."*

THE END

Your Financial Journey Continues

Congratulations! You've just invested in yourself and the future of your business. I'm confident that will pay off. True financial transformation doesn't end with closing this book—it begins.

To support your ongoing journey toward financial confidence, I've created three pathways to help you implement what you've learned:

1. Resources at Your Fingertips

Visit our dedicated resource center at www.finforfounders.com to access:

- Customizable financial planning templates
- Comprehensive budgeting spreadsheets
- Our proprietary financial assessment tools to establish your current position and set realistic goals
- Step-by-step checklists for each strategy covered in this book

These tools transform concepts into concrete action plans tailored to your unique situation.

2. AI-Powered Guidance

Have a specific question as you implement these strategies? Our AI assistant is available 24/7 to provide instant clarification on any concept from the book. Whether you're wondering about how to calculate a financial ratio or need help interpreting financial statements, simply ask and receive personalized guidance based on the principles we've discussed.

Access this feature at https://finforfounders.com/ai-assistant or scan the QR code below.

3. Expert-Level Support

If you recognize that you need some help, Fintelligent is here for you. We provide all the finance team services that we discussed in the book, on an easy, outsourced basis. So, if you're looking for your very own "Mike," please visit www.fintelligent.com to learn more.

Our team provides services like the Four Pillars you just read about, including:

- **Accounting:** Virtual Accounting to handle day-to-day accounting tasks
- **Reporting:** Included in all our subscriptions
- **Planning & Analysis:** Virtual Analysis subscriptions providing an annual plan, customized KPIs, and an analyst to interpret and maintain your metrics.
- **Advice:** Our Virtual CFO subscription provides a seasoned financial executive providing strategic guidance to grow your company. Includes Virtual Analysis services.

All our subscriptions offer add-ons to customize your experience and help you make smarter financial decisions! You can access more detail about our subscriptions at https://fintelligent.com/subscriptions or by scanning the QR code below.

Remember, financial freedom isn't a destination—it's an ongoing practice. The principles in this book have transformed countless businesses, and I'm committed to supporting you as you write your own success story.

To your financial future,
Rob Ripp

www.ingramcontent.com/pod-product-compliance
Lightning Source LLC
Chambersburg PA
CBHW071726200326
41519CB00021BC/6594